WHY GOD LETS US CHOOSE

STEPHEN D. NADAULD

WHY GOD LETS US CHOOSE

How Agency Explains the Way Life Works

MM.®

**DESERET
BOOK**

SALT LAKE CITY, UTAH

Two roads diverged in a wood, and I—
I took the one less traveled by,
And that has made all the difference.

—Robert Frost

Library of Congress Cataloging-in-Publication Data

Nadauld, Stephen Douglas.
    Why God lets us choose : how agency explains the way life works / Stephen D. Nadauld.
        p. cm.
    Includes bibliographical references and index.
    ISBN 978-1-60641-030-1 (hardbound : alk. paper)
    1. Free will and determinism—Religious aspects—Church of Jesus Christ of Latter-day Saints.   2. Spiritual life—Church of Jesus Christ of Latter-day Saints.   3. Church of Jesus Christ of Latter-day Saints—Doctrines.   I. Title.
    BX8643.F69N34 2009
    234'.9—dc22   2008046888

Printed in the United States of America
Sheridan Books, Chelsea, MI

10   9   8   7   6   5   4   3   2   1

Contents

CHAPTER ONE

Agency: The First Gift

A CLOSE EXAMINATION of the scriptures reveals that God our Heavenly Father gave us, His children, two great gifts. The second was the gift of His Son to be a savior and redeemer. That second gift was a complement to, and was made necessary by, the first—the gift of agency. Without the promise of the second gift, that we could be redeemed from Adam's transgression as well as our own, we may not have accepted the first gift. This book is about the Father's first great gift—the gift of agency.

I began thinking more seriously about the gift of agency as Sister Nadauld and I recently presided over the Switzerland Geneva Mission. Prior to our call we had raised seven sons and observed them as they made choices and exercised their agency. We spoke often (and longingly, I might add) in those childrearing days of the notion known as "agency and how to enforce it." We recognized that agency is an important principle in God's economy, but we wished we could abrogate or suspend it for a season. We hoped to forestall as long as possible the graying of our hair, the wrinkling of our skin, and the possible losing of our minds. We somehow survived the trauma of seven teenaged sons, although we clearly didn't escape some of the aforementioned effects.

Along the way we also experienced firsthand another concept: "agency and how to recover from it" (as expressed by a dear friend). Choices have outcomes or consequences that often require "recovering from." The salvage operations that follow the exercise of agency teach much about how to improve decision making in the future. These salvage operations also teach us about the blessings of the atonement and the extraordinary love of the Father and His Son for the Father's children. Without that love and atonement, "recovering from" would not be possible.

Wonderfully enough, my wife and I were blessed with magnificent missionaries whose exercise of agency and strict obedience were motivated by their love of the Savior. We once heard a mission president's assignment compared to being a Boy Scout leader on a three-year campout. Such a description was funny, but we also saw it as demeaning—and it didn't fit with our experience. We thought of our missionaries as heroes whose young and eager feet were beautiful feet upon the mountains, bringing the gospel to the people of Switzerland and France. They were extraordinary in every way, angelic in their countenances, determined in their step, and filled with goodness in their hearts. And we loved them dearly. Their exercise of agency and their obedience to gospel principles were extraordinary. But they were faced on a daily basis with a barrage of questions from those who did not have knowledge of important gospel principles.

A Few of Life's Questions

Our missionaries heard questions about life that no doubt have been asked in one form or another through the millennia. "If there is a God, why would He allow _____?" Depending on the person and their circumstances, that blank could be filled in with war, famine, cruelty, poverty, death, destruction, suffering, or a variety of other troubles. Or the question might be, "Why do the wicked prosper, or why do bad things happen to good people?" The missionaries responded to these questions as best they could.

They would then come to us with questions of their own. Why won't Sister Dupont be baptized, since she knows our message is true? Or if Brother Chavalier would only exercise faith he would be able to make progress. Why can't he see that? Or, President, why can't the Holy Ghost speak with a louder voice? Or why can't I make Sister Lambert feel the same spirit I feel when I read the Book of Mormon? Veiled in each of these questions is the larger issue: Why does God let us choose?

As I thought about these questions, along with some of my own, I realized that often the answers are somehow connected to the principle of agency. Agency helps explain why we are here and where we are going. It explains what happened in the Garden of Eden. It explains much of life's injustices and uncertainties. Agency plays an important role in the gaining of wisdom and judgment. It explains how we are to learn by study and also by faith. It explains why the Holy Ghost speaks with a still small voice.

As I studied and thought about other questions, I realized that agency often provides answers to them as well. After further pondering, I concluded that our understanding of gospel principles is enhanced in an extraordinary way when we fully appreciate how pervasive the influence of agency is.

What Is Agency?

In the simplest sense, agency can be thought of as having choices or alternatives. Implicit in the concept of agency is that choices are not only available, but we must be free to choose between them. (That freedom of choice often leads us to use the term *free agency*. But as we'll discuss later, the scriptures don't speak of free agency; the Lord's terminology is *moral agency*.)

That understanding of agency as having freedom of choice, though valid, is still incomplete. As a gospel principle that is integral to our Heavenly Father's plan, agency actually contains four essential elements: (1) The existence of an intelligent or conscious being, (2) knowledge of a standard and consequences, (3) a choice between alternatives, and (4) freedom of choice. (I appreciate my university colleague Craig Merrill's contribution to my thinking about these four elements.)

Consider the first requirement: the existence of an intelligent being. In latter-day revelation we learn, "Man was also in the beginning with God. Intelligence, or the light of truth, was not created or made, neither indeed can be" (D&C 93:29). And in the book of Abraham we read, "If there be two spirits, and one shall be more intelligent than the other, yet these two spirits . . . have no beginning; they existed before, they shall have no end, they shall exist after" (Abraham 3:18).

All of God's spirit children, in any sphere, are intelligences that existed with God from the beginning. It is safe to presume that such intelligences are capable of conscious thought and are able to process information and to use that capability to come to rational conclusions. The logic is straightforward. The existence of choice is meaningless without a chooser or agent. And agency or choice is instituted to benefit the intelligent beings who will be making the choices. This idea is amplified in Doctrine and Covenants 93:31, which states, "Behold, here is the agency of man, and here is the condemnation of man; because that which was from the beginning is plainly manifest unto them, and they receive not the light."

As hard as it sometimes is to believe, our children are and always have been intelligent beings. They were intelligences in the premortal world, capable of conscious thought, and able to process information and to arrive at correct conclusions. Indeed, it may be that many of them were and will be more intelligent and capable than we. How useful it is to remember that as we attempt to teach them about agency here on earth.

The second element of agency is knowledge. In the book of Moses we read, "The Lord said unto Enoch: Behold these thy brethren; they are the workmanship of mine own hands, and I gave unto them their knowledge, in the day I created them; and in the Garden of Eden, gave I unto man his agency" (Moses 7:32). From the beginning the Lord has provided knowledge of standards (commandments) and of consequences in order for the exercise of agency to be more than just a roll of the dice. In other words, *un*informed choice between alternatives can be made with a toss of a coin or the roll of a die. But one of the reasons God gave man agency was to allow the development of wisdom and judgment. Wisdom and judgment are the result of careful analysis and selection among alternatives based on knowledge of outcomes and consequences. Agency was not meant to describe a process of successive choices that is navigated by means of a random number-generator.

Knowledge is critical to the exercise of agency. Children who learn correct principles from their parents are greatly blessed. Parents and all others who learn correct principles from the prophets and apostles are also greatly blessed. God has revealed true principles to prophets in every dispensation in order to bless

His earthly children with the knowledge they need to properly exercise agency.

The third element of agency is the one most naturally associated with the concept. Agency does not exist in any meaningful sense unless there are alternatives among which one can choose. A plan that does away with alternatives, such as that proposed by the devil, destroys the concept of agency. This truth was taught to Moses:

> And I, the Lord God, spake unto Moses, saying: That Satan, whom thou hast commanded in the name of mine Only Begotten, is the same which was from the beginning, and he came before me, saying—Behold, here am I, send me, I will be thy son, and I will redeem all mankind, that one soul shall not be lost, and surely I will do it; wherefore give me thine honor.
>
> But, behold, my Beloved Son, which was my Beloved and Chosen from the beginning, said unto me—Father, thy will be done, and the glory be thine forever.
>
> Wherefore, because that Satan rebelled against me, and sought *to destroy the agency of man,* which I, the Lord God, had given him, and also, that I should give unto him mine own power; by the power of mine Only Begotten, I caused that he should be cast down. (Moses 4:1–3; emphasis added)

In verse 1 Satan proposes that "I will redeem all mankind, that one soul shall not be lost, and surely I will do it." The implication is clear. Satan would allow no alternative or choice to any soul. God understood the proposal and stated succinctly in verse 3 that Satan "sought to destroy the agency of man, which I, the Lord God, had *given* him." God would not allow that agency, His first great gift to man, should be taken away or destroyed and caused that Satan "should be cast down." God's intent was to preserve for man the gift of alternatives and choice.

It is critical to appreciate that the concept of alternatives necessarily includes the notion of outcomes or consequences. Consequences are inextricably connected to choices. In the vernacular, it is said that one cannot pick up one end of the stick (choices) without picking up the other (consequences).

The fourth element of agency is perhaps implicit and need not be stated except to finalize the logic. Logic suggests that even if choices exist, agency is not operative unless one is free or unconstrained by external forces to actually make a choice. Perhaps this is where the idea of *free* agency comes from. Attaching the word *free* to concepts of choice and agency makes it explicit that choosing among alternatives must be unconstrained—but that attachment causes other problems. It turns out that freedom of choice or free agency as it is construed in our modern society is not exactly what God had in mind for His children.

To summarize the four elements of agency: agency exists when intelligent (conscious) beings, with knowledge of standards and consequences, are allowed to choose among alternatives and outcomes without external constraints. We will see how this expanded notion of agency comes into play in future chapters.

Why Understand Agency?

Growing in understanding of agency isn't just an intellectual exercise. As we come to a more complete understanding of the gift and principle of agency, we will better understand why God lets us choose and better be able to explain what we experience during our earthly sojourn. And better understanding often leads to better behavior. President Boyd K. Packer's profound observation applies directly in this context. He said, "The study of the doctrines of the gospel will improve behavior quicker than talking about behavior will improve behavior" ("Washed Clean," *Ensign*, May 1997, 9).

Keep in mind, then, that while it is a good thing to have explanations and to gain understanding, there is something more to be hoped for as we explore the gift of agency. We should ask, what is it God hoped we would do with our great gift?

An answer to that question becomes clear when we consider the poignant passages found in the book of Moses that describe a conversation between Enoch and God. We read, "And Enoch beheld angels descending out of heaven, bearing testimony of the Father and Son; and the Holy Ghost fell on many, and they were caught up by the powers of heaven into Zion" (Moses 7:27).

Any parent who has anticipated the coming home of a child can imagine how our Heavenly Father must have felt as He saw many of His righteous children returning to His and their heavenly home. There was undoubtedly great rejoicing, as is present in any reunion between loved ones. Our contemplation of the sweetness of such reunions provides a dramatic backdrop for what happens next. The next verses explain:

> And it came to pass that the God of heaven looked upon the residue of the people, and he wept; and Enoch bore record of it, saying: How is it that the heavens weep, and shed forth their tears as the rain upon the mountains?
> And Enoch said unto the Lord: How is it that thou canst weep, seeing thou art holy, and from all eternity to all eternity? (Moses 7:28–29)

Enoch is clearly perplexed. Hadn't God just welcomed home many of His spirit children? Why, as He looked upon the residue of the people, would He weep? Enoch could not immediately understand why someone who was holy and whose power and understanding spread from "all eternity to all eternity" would be found weeping.

In his struggle to comprehend, Enoch continues to rehearse some of what he knows about God as additional context to his astonishment. We read in verse 30, "And were it possible that man could number the particles of the earth, yea, millions of earths like this, it would not be a beginning to the number of thy creations; and thy curtains are stretched out still; and yet thou art there, and thy bosom is there; and also thou art just; thou art merciful and kind forever" (Moses 7:30).

Enoch not only reviews the vastness of God's physical creations but also pauses to remind himself of the vastness of God's other attributes, such as justice, mercy, and kindness. He then continues, "And thou hast taken Zion to thine own bosom, from all thy creations, from all eternity to all eternity; and naught but peace, justice, and truth is the habitation of thy throne; and mercy shall go before thy face and have no end; how is it thou canst weep?" (Moses 7:31).

From Enoch's perspective, an all-powerful, all-knowing God, whose attributes include peace, justice, truth, and mercy, should have no conceivable reason ever to weep or ever to be sad. In modern vernacular, we might think of Enoch as saying, You are a huge success! You have cars, houses, and money. You are good and wise and kind. Why would you be unhappy?

God's answer should give us powerful reason to pause and contemplate. "The Lord said unto Enoch: Behold these thy brethren; they are the workmanship of mine own hands, and I gave unto them their knowledge, in the day I created them; and in the Garden of Eden, gave I unto man his agency" (Moses 7:32).

God is explaining to Enoch that all those who were not taken up into His bosom are also the workmanship of His own hands.

They are His children whom He had created, to whom He had given knowledge, and to whom He had given the incomparable gift of agency. The implication is clearly that He cares about them and loves them. God's love for His children and His desire to see them all come home to Him makes the final verses especially poignant. God says, "And unto thy brethren have I said, and also given commandment, that they should love one another, *and that they should choose me, their Father;* but behold, they are without affection, and they hate their own blood" (Moses 7:33; emphasis added).

Now it is clear why God has wept. He has only one desire for His children. He has created them, endowed them with knowledge, and given them agency. He desires only that they *choose Him,* their Father. He wants only that those children whom He loves so much return that affection and choose to love Him back. And when they choose to be *without* affection for Him or for their own children, He has cause to weep.

How like God the Father are we as earthly parents. We may have possessions, status, and influence in large or small measure, but we weep when our children choose not to follow our counsel or return our love. And we weep more when those children choose not to love the Lord or follow His counsel.

It is good to understand the marvelous gift of agency. It is useful to appreciate how much of what we observe can be explained by agency. It is insightful to realize how integral agency is to our mortal existence. But it is particularly important to actually experience the gift in the right way. My hope in writing these things is that agency will be better understood—but, more important, I pray that it will be better used. I pray that we will use the gift God gave us and choose Him, that we will choose to follow His Son, and that all of our choices will lead us back to our heavenly home from whence we came.

CHAPTER TWO

Agency and Premortality

I T IS THE NATURE of mankind to want an explanation of things.
It starts at an early age. Daddy, why is ice cold? Mommy, why
are your eyes brown? Parents usually arrive at acceptable answers
to their children's questions. But the answers to some questions
have been sought through the ages and have occupied the attention of the world's greatest minds. This is underscored by a fascinating paragraph from a book review that recently appeared in
Scientific American. The reviewer was referring to the difficulty
that modern physicists are having as they try to explain how the
forces of nature can be reconciled into one grand "theory of everything." Since Einstein, physicists have been attempting to discover
how the theory of relativity, quantum mechanics, and other modern theories can be tied together. By their own admission they have
not had much success.

In his book review, George Johnson observes, "Most theorists reject this postmodern fatalism, hoping for the breakthrough that points the way to the mountain top. Gathering in Beijing this summer for the Spring 2006 conference they packed the Great Hall of the People to hear Stephen Hawking declare: 'We are close to answering an age-old question. *Why are we here? Where did we come from?*'" (*Scientific American,* September 2006, 120; emphasis added).

How interesting! As Latter-day Saints, for years we have been telling people we have answers to life's three great questions: Where did we come from? Why are we here? Where are we going? But the great scientists of the world continue to ponder and debate those same age-old questions. Today they still pursue the answer to their questions through mathematical models, scientific experiments, and trial and error. Certainly their efforts sometimes lead to insights that improve our understanding and benefit mankind. However, as Latter-day Saints we have information available to us that is of inestimable value to those who seek answers to the important questions of life.

In reflecting on that available information, I was struck one day by two thoughts. The first was obvious, but the other was an insight I hadn't considered before. The obvious thought was that all available information concerning our premortal existence comes from the scriptures and latter-day prophets. We have no personal experience to draw from—at least none that we can remember. We must rely completely on the amount and kind of information that the Lord felt would be in our best interest. The best of that information has only recently been made available as we have been blessed with the Book of Mormon, Doctrine and Covenants, Pearl of Great Price, and revelations to modern prophets and apostles. Such is the blessing of living in the time of the restoration of all things.

The more interesting insight concerns the *nature* of the information that has been made available. Many topics relating to our premortal lives could be of interest. Who were our friends? How did we travel? What did we eat—or did we eat at all? What did we do all day? Did we listen to music, climb mountains, have a favorite team? The list of questions is limited only by our imagination. It's interesting that we really don't know anything about any of these topics.

Instead, one of the rare pieces of information we have about premortality has to do with *agency*. That should tell us something. Not only is agency inherently interesting, but we should take special note of God's view of what is important for us to understand.

What We Know of Premortality

Let us examine what we know about our premortal estate and the role that agency played in that sphere. Before coming to earth, we existed as spirit children of loving heavenly parents. Of that premortal existence Elder Bruce R. McConkie observed, "Speaking of this prior existence in a spirit sphere, the First Presidency of the Church (Joseph F. Smith, John R. Winder, and Anthon H. Lund) said: 'All men and women are in the similitude *of the universal Father and Mother,* and are literally the sons and daughters of Deity'; as spirits they were the 'offspring of *celestial parentage'*" (Joseph Fielding Smith, *Man: His Origin and Destiny* [Salt Lake City: Deseret Book, 1954], 351, 355; in Bruce R. McConkie, *Mormon Doctrine,* 2nd ed. [Salt Lake City: Bookcraft, 1966], 589; emphasis in original).

As suggested earlier, we know little of the activities we experienced with our heavenly family. But we do know of one very significant event that took place. In heaven we experienced war. We read in the book of Revelation:

> And there was war in heaven: Michael and his angels fought against the dragon; and the dragon fought and his

angels, and prevailed not; neither was their place found any more in heaven. And the great dragon was cast out, that old serpent, called the Devil, and Satan, which deceiveth the whole world: he was cast out into the earth, and his angels were cast out with him. (Revelation 12:7–9)

Additional descriptions of this event are found in Revelation 12:4–13 (Joseph Smith Translation), Isaiah 14:12, and Doctrine and Covenants 29:36–38.

Why the conflict? Why this war in heaven? Moses 4 gives us a clear answer. Verse 1 explains that Satan, who was a spirit son of God, came before the Father and presented a plan for redeeming all mankind. The salient feature of his plan was that "one soul shall not be lost" (Moses 4:1). But saving every soul was not his altruistic aim. He wanted the glory, honor, and power of the Father. In short, he rebelled against the Father. We read, "Wherefore, because that Satan rebelled against me, and sought *to destroy the agency of man, which I, the Lord God, had given him,* and also, that I should give unto him mine own power; by the power of mine Only Begotten, I caused that he should be cast down" (Moses 4:3; emphasis added). We find in this and previous verses the three principal reasons for the war in heaven. The war was fought over conflicting plans for the redemption of mankind, over who should be the redeemer and ultimately receive the glory and power associated with that redemption, and over whether or not man would retain his agency. Verse 3 makes it very clear that agency was a gift given directly to man from God and that God was not willing that it be taken away or destroyed.

Agency was God's first great gift to man. It is obvious from our earthly experience that a more powerful person can impose his will on a less powerful person. That imposition can come as physical, emotional, or mental force or restraint. God, as the most intelligent of all (see Abraham 3:19), could have devised a way to subjugate all other spirits to His will. He chose not to. Rather, He chose to give to man the incomparable gift of agency. How remarkable!

The agency of man was not just a passing fancy, a gift that was given lightly and could be reconsidered. Indeed, our Heavenly Father lost fully one-third of His spirit children over the issue of agency. The importance of this extraordinary gift to the plan of redemption and to an understanding of our experiences here on the earth cannot be overstated.

We gain some insight concerning agency, the plan of redemption, and the nature of our choices from the book of Alma. After explaining that the plan of redemption "was laid from the foundation of the world" (Alma 12:25), Alma describes the nature of premortal choices made by those who would be ordained high priests after the order of the Son of God. He explains in Alma 13:3 that those individuals were "prepared from the foundation of the world . . . on account of their exceeding faith and good works; in the first place being left to choose good or evil; therefore they having chosen good, and exercising exceedingly great faith, are called with a holy calling."

These brethren distinguished themselves in two ways. First, they were known for their faith—even their "exceedingly great faith"—and second, they were known for their good works. They exercised their agency, made premortal choices between good and evil, and as a result qualified for greater blessings to come. Their faith was a belief both that the Father's plan would work and that the Father's eldest son would fulfill the role of Savior and Redeemer as envisioned in the plan. Their good works would have involved defending the plan and teaching others of its merits. They testified that Jesus Christ would surely do all that He said He would do. We can safely assume that they taught and testified of their faith that Christ would come to earth and shed His own blood to atone for the sins of all mankind.

To have faith and to support the plan were conscious choices. Those choices were a direct exercise of the agency given to them by the Father. At the same time, other spirits exercised their agency by choosing *not* to accept the Father's plan. They chose not to believe that the plan would work. They could not be convinced that Jehovah would condescend to leave His exalted position in the heavens and be born in a stable, live through the pains and suffering of mortality and ultimately allow Himself to be crucified for the sins of the world. Or they felt that if Jehovah did so condescend, they were not convinced that He would be successful in His mission.

Satan's Opposition

What arguments could have been made by Satan that would have caused one-third of the hosts of heaven to make the wrong choice? Of course we can only surmise, but the arguments may have a familiar ring.

One major issue almost certainly would have been the understanding that a wrong choice on earth could have potentially serious spiritual consequences. We understood that our Heavenly Father was a God of justice and that the laws of justice would be in force during our earthly sojourn. We knew punishments would be associated with our mistakes and violations of God's law. For some kinds of mistakes those punishments would be severe, even so severe that we could forfeit our eternal inheritance. That was understandably a frightening proposition and surely caused some to believe we could not do it. Knowing that we would not always choose wisely, some felt the consequences were too frightening and therefore did not want the responsibility of choice or agency—it was just too hard!

Satan played on our fears. He sympathized with our worry that it would be too hard. He agreed that the punishments would be too harsh and that there was a chance we would fail miserably. He said his plan would solve the problem of making costly mistakes. We would not have to fear; he would make sure that there would be no punishment and that we would all succeed.

When it was pointed out that God's plan involved forgiveness of mistakes through an atoning sacrifice, Satan said it was too complicated. He said there was a strong possibility we would live our whole lives and never hear about that part of the plan. And he kept returning to the argument that we could not be sure the plan would work. He said no one would be willing to endure the incalculable suffering that would be associated with the combined sins of all who would come to earth.

Furthermore he said we would experience sorrow and sadness during the whole earthly process. We would be miserable not only because we would make mistakes, but also because we would be hurt by the mistakes of others.

Satan argued that we couldn't succeed, we would constantly be upset, we would fail, the plan would not work, and we were right to be afraid. The solution was to forfeit our agency, put away our fears, and let him give us a guarantee. His would be a lifetime, money-back guarantee—a no cost, no fear, no punishment, no sorrow, no sadness guarantee. All we had to do was politely refuse the gift of agency. We would give it back. After all it was just a Pandora's box. It contained all the ills, plagues, troubles, trials, and miseries we would find in the world.

These arguments of Satan were appealing. They were probably first introduced as talking points. The talking points led to lively discussions, then to heated discussions, and then to angry debates. The process became so bitter, so severe, that it could be adequately described only as a war—the war in heaven. It was a war fought over conflicting plans for redemption, over who would be in charge, and over the gift of agency.

The result was a great division of the hosts of heaven. Two-thirds took one side in the war; one-third took the other. The war was not a conventional war with tanks and planes and artillery. It was a war of ideas and concepts. It was fought over two different visions for the future experiences and ultimate outcomes of the spirit children of God.

How the War in Heaven Was Won

The book of Revelation provides a wonderful insight into how the upper hand was gained in this great premortal conflict.

> And there was war in heaven; Michael and his angels fought against the dragon; and the dragon and his angels fought against Michael; and the dragon prevailed not against Michael, neither the child, nor the woman which was the church of God, who had been delivered of her pains, and brought forth the kingdom of our God and his Christ. Neither was there place found in heaven for the great dragon, who was cast out; that old serpent called the devil, and also called Satan, which deceiveth the whole world; he was cast out into the earth; and his angels were cast out with him.
>
> And I heard a loud voice saying in heaven, Now is come salvation, and strength, and the kingdom of our God, and the power of his Christ; for the accuser of our brethren is cast down, which accused them before our God day and night. For they have overcome *him by the blood of the Lamb,* and by the *word of their testimony;* for they loved not their own lives, but kept the testimony even unto death. Therefore, rejoice O heavens, and ye that dwell in them. (JST, Revelation 12:6–11; emphasis added)

The great premortal conflict was won not by force or by abrogating agency but by *testifying* that an atonement would be wrought by the shedding of the blood of Christ. Assurances were given that Christ would fulfill His role in the plan. The fears promoted by Satan and his followers were overcome by the faith and testimony of Michael and his hosts. Agency was not to be feared but embraced. Mistakes made on earth could be forgiven, and the punishments affixed would be paid for by the suffering and spilt blood of Jesus Christ, Savior and Redeemer of all mankind.

In the end, the polar positions of fear and faith were incompatible; they could not coexist. God exercised His power and separated the two opposing forces. Satan and the one-third who followed him were "cast out." They became the devil and his angels. The "casting out" did not end the war. It was in some sense only the beginning. The war in heaven was the first great battle in a long protracted struggle. The devil *has not conceded defeat.* He is still fighting a war.

Our Choices in Premortality

As the battle goes on around us in mortality, we would do well to employ the strategy that was successful in our first estate. Faith in the atoning sacrifice of Christ will allow us to overcome our fears, our sorrows, and our sins. Faith will allow us to access the blessings of the atonement and give us strength to keep the commandments of God. Teaching faith to our children and encouraging them to love the Lord will help alleviate our fears as they exercise their agency. How great will be our joy when they and we together choose to follow the Savior.

We who comprised the two-thirds, who opted to retain the gift of agency and submit to the plan of redemption proposed by the Father and His Son, Jesus Christ, are those who have had, are having, and will have an experience in mortality. We have exercised our agency; we have basically chosen to keep choosing. Our experience in mortality is all about choices. It is all about understanding the gift of agency and the sickness and health, the joy and sorrow, the highs and lows and ultimate triumph that our Heavenly Father intended that we experience.

Just as choices made in mortality have consequences, it is not unreasonable to suppose that choices made in our premortality might also have had various outcomes. The result of choosing God's plan in premortality is our opportunity to come to earth and experience all that is inherent in that choice. But is there more to it than that?

We previously noted an important teaching of Alma from the Book of Mormon. He taught that certain priesthood callings in mortality were a result of the faith and good works exhibited in premortality. A similar principle is put forth in the book of Abraham:

> Now the Lord had shown unto me, Abraham, the intelligences that were organized before the world was; and among all these there were many of the noble and great ones;
>
> And God saw these souls that they were good, and he stood in the midst of them, and he said: These I will make my rulers; for he stood among those that were spirits, and he saw that they were good; and he said unto me: Abraham, thou art one of them; thou wast chosen before thou wast born. (Abraham 3:22–23)

Abraham and others were identified by God as "noble and great" and "that they were good." In Doctrine and Covenants 138, President Joseph F. Smith also speaks of leaders of past dispensations and the present dispensation as being among the noble and

great ones who "received their first lessons in the world of spirits
and were prepared to come forth in the due time of the Lord"
(D&C 138:56).

These references suggest that choices made and behaviors
exhibited in the premortal sphere explain callings and responsibilities of both men and women in this mortal existence. But if the
exercise of agency in premortality explains why some are leaders on
earth, does premortal agency also explain other circumstances of
our earthly experience? Does it explain why some are born into
poverty or with physical disabilities or in some other circumstance
generally viewed as undesirable?

Concerning these questions, President Harold B. Lee made
the following wise observation:

> Between the extremes of the "noble and great" spirits,
> whom God would make his rulers (see Abraham 3:22–23),
> and the disobedient and the rebellious who were cast out
> with Satan, there were obviously many spirits with varying
> degrees of faithfulness. May we not assume from these
> teachings that the progress and development we made as
> spirits have brought privileges and blessings here according
> to our faithfulness in the spirit world? Now don't be too
> hasty in your conclusions as to what conditions in mortal-
> ity constitute the greater privileges. That condition in life
> which gives the greatest experience and opportunity for
> development is the one to be most desired and anyone so
> privileged is most favored of God. It has been said that "a
> smooth sea never made a skillful mariner"; neither do
> uninterrupted prosperity and success qualify for usefulness
> and happiness. The storms of adversity, like those of the
> ocean, rouse the faculties and excite the invention, pru-
> dence, skill and fortitude of the voyager. The mariners of

ancient times, in bracing their minds to outward calamities, acquired a loftiness of purpose and a moral heroism worth a lifetime of softness and security. (*Teachings of Harold B. Lee* [Salt Lake City: Bookcraft, 1996], 23)

President Lee's point is clear. Premortal agency explains some of what we observe in mortality, but we would be wise to heed his injunction to not "be too hasty in your conclusions as to what conditions in mortality constitute the greater privileges."

We can now answer Stephen Hawking's question, Why are we here? Because we chose to come. We exercised the gift of agency given by God and made the deliberate choice to follow His plan. We are not here by happenstance. We are not here because an event with some infinitesimally small probability of occurrence resulted in the creation of the earth and all its inhabitants. We are here by choice! And, contrary to some popularly held notions, we should be happy to be here. The potential rewards are enormous. We are promised an inheritance with our heavenly parents in a celestialized world if we can learn to wisely exercise the gift of agency.

In our premortal existence, when presented with a choice of plans for our future happiness, we made the right one! We chose wisely and well. We should take confidence from that knowledge. We should go forward in faith and not fear. We should proceed with the strength that comes from knowing that we did it right once and can keep doing it right in the future. Agency explains why we are here. We chose to come. Hurrah for us!

CHAPTER THREE

Agency in the Garden of Eden

F EW STORIES HAVE evoked as much curiosity and interest as that of Adam and Eve in the Garden of Eden. Writers, artists, poets, and humorists have been fascinated by conditions in the garden and have produced a great number of works describing what they imagined went on there. As an example, consider a statement by Mark Twain. In 1901 Mark Twain (Samuel Clemens) appeared before a committee that was holding a public hearing on a bill that would license osteopaths in the state of New York. His purpose was to support the osteopaths, and his argument was that the people should have the liberty or agency to make their own health-care decisions. The following was reported in the February 28, 1901, edition of the *New York Times*:

> I believe we ought to retain all of our liberties. We can't afford to throw any of them away. They didn't come to us

in a night, like Jonah's gourd, if Jonah was the man who had a gourd. [Laughter.] The moment you start to drive anybody out of the state, then you have the same situation which existed in the Garden of Eden. I don't know as I cared much about the osteopaths until I heard you were going to drive them out of the state, but since I heard that I haven't been able to sleep. [Laughter.]

I suppose if you do drive them out, they will go up to Vermont, which has been characterized here as the 'garbage ground of the profession,' and which, since it became that, has also become one of the healthiest states in the union, and I suppose I can go up there without much trouble. But anyhow, it worries me. I can conceive just how it was in the Garden of Eden when the Lord told Adam he must not eat of the forbidden fruit. And my own opinion is that Adam is unjustly criticized. I am confident that if any of my tribe had been in the Garden of Eden when that injunction was served they never would have contented themselves with just one apple. They would have eaten the whole crop. [Great laughter.]

Twain was certainly deft at using humor to make a point. On another occasion, he made the observation, "Adam was but human—this explains it all. He did not want the apple for the apple's sake, he wanted it only because it was forbidden. The mistake was in not forbidding the serpent; then he would have eaten the serpent" (*Pudd'nhead Wilson* [New York: Bantam Classics, 1984], 6).

Of course, we don't read Mark Twain for doctrinal insight. But he, with us, recognized that man's first experience with agency in mortality occurred in that setting. We can improve on Twain's understanding of what occurred in the garden by taking advantage of scriptures that have come forth in this last dispensation.

A very clear account of events in the garden is found in the Pearl of Great Price. After reading a description of the various steps in the creation, we read in Moses 3:7, "And I, the Lord God, formed man from the dust of the ground, and breathed into his nostrils the breath of life; and man became a living soul." Further, in verse 15 we read, "And I, the Lord God, took the man, and put him into the Garden of Eden, to dress it, and to keep it."

According to the account in the book of Moses, the man (Adam) had barely set his feet on the ground of the garden when the issue of agency arose. The narrative continues: "And I, the Lord God, commanded the man, saying: Of every tree of the garden thou mayest freely eat, but of the tree of the knowledge of good and evil, thou shalt not eat of it, *nevertheless, thou mayest choose for thyself, for it is given unto thee;* but, remember that I forbid it, for in the day thou eatest thereof thou shalt surely die" (Moses 3:16–17; emphasis added).

These verses reaffirm two salient points we have observed before. First, we were meant to have the freedom of choice. We had it in the premortal world, and now it would be a defining characteristic of life in mortality. Second, agency is a gift of God. As the Lord says, "thou mayest choose . . . *for it is given unto thee.*" In this same book of Moses, as noted in the previous chapter, the war in heaven was fought "because that Satan rebelled against me, and *sought to destroy the agency of man, which I, the Lord God, had given him*" (Moses 4:3; emphasis added).

Agency is clearly a gift given to man by God. One of the first concepts Adam was taught by God was that "*thou mayest choose for thyself.*" But immediately after being made aware that he could choose, he was also told that it was forbidden for him to choose to obtain a knowledge of good and evil. We may wonder if in fact the prohibition was not meant to be permanent but only temporary. Perhaps in due time it would be rescinded and Adam could obtain the knowledge of good and evil after having been duly authorized by God.

But now things really get interesting for Adam. He is not left to ponder for long his opportunity to exercise agency. Only a few verses later we read:

> And I, the Lord God, caused a deep sleep to fall upon Adam; and he slept, and I took one of his ribs and closed up the flesh in the stead thereof;
>
> And the rib which I, the Lord God, had taken from man, made I a woman, and brought her unto the man.
>
> And Adam said: This I know now is bone of my bones, and flesh of my flesh; and she shall be called Woman, because she was taken out of man.
>
> Therefore shall a man leave his father and his mother, and shall cleave unto his wife; and they shall be one flesh. (Moses 3:21–24)

Adam was now no longer alone in the garden. He had company. He had a companion. His choices would not just affect him, but they would also impact this new companion. And as he was soon to discover, choices made by the companion could also have a dramatic impact on him.

We read earlier that Satan, who had been "cast down," appeared in the form of a serpent in the garden. The book of Moses explains what happened next:

> And Satan put it into the heart of the serpent, (for he had drawn away many after him,) and he [Satan] sought

also to beguile Eve, *for he knew not the mind of God,* wherefore he sought to destroy the world.

And he said unto the woman: Yea, hath God said—Ye shall not eat of every tree of the garden? (And he spake by the mouth of the serpent.)

And the woman said unto the serpent: We may eat of the fruit of the trees of the garden; but of the fruit of the tree which thou beholdest in the midst of the garden, God hath said—Ye shall not eat of it, neither shall ye touch it, lest ye die.

And the serpent said unto the woman: Ye shall not surely die; for God doth know that in the day ye eat thereof, then your eyes shall be opened, and ye shall be as gods, knowing good and evil.

And when the woman saw that the tree was good for food, and that it became pleasant to the eyes, *and a tree to be desired to make her wise,* she took of the fruit thereof, and did eat, and also gave unto her husband with her, and he did eat. (Moses 4:6–11; emphasis added)

These verses are intriguing for a number of reasons. Concerning the phrase, "*for he knew not the mind of God,*" we could ask, did Satan not remember the plan of redemption endorsed by the firstborn Son of God? Did he not understand the role he would be playing in that plan? Did he seek "to destroy the world" believing that he would be successful in thwarting the plan that he had so violently opposed? Was he seeking to usurp the authority of God by taking charge of the events that were to unfold in the garden? We do not know.

But we do learn that Eve was given to understand that a knowledge of good and evil would cause her and Adam to "*be as gods*" and that the tree of knowledge of good and evil was "*a tree to be desired to make her wise.*" To be as the gods, and to be wise—for these very good reasons Eve exercised her agency and chose to eat of the fruit. This was clearly part of the plan of God. It was intended that God's spirit children come to the earth to obtain wisdom, to learn to choose between good and evil, and to become more godlike in the process.

Did Eve make her choice with a full understanding of all the implications of that choice? Had Satan not tempted Eve would God have authorized the partaking of the fruit in order for the plan to go forth? We do not know.

We do know that after Eve exercised her agency, it was still left to Adam to exercise his. How much discussion and analysis were involved we are not told but are left to ponder. We do know that Adam chose to "cleave unto his wife" and to experience with her the obtaining of wisdom, the understanding of good and evil, and becoming as the gods that were consequences of his decision.

The Plan of Joy

The result of the joint choices of Adam and Eve was the unfolding of the plan of God. "The eyes of them both were opened" (Moses 4:13). "And I, the Lord God, said unto mine Only Begotten: Behold, the man is become as one of us to know good and evil" (Moses 4:28). Adam and Eve left the state of innocence they knew in the garden and became mortal. They were cast out of the garden into the world as we know it—a world of joy and sorrow, of pleasure and pain, of righteousness and sin—in short, a world designed to be a testing place where we could learn wisdom and judgment according to the plan of God. After having spent some time in mortality, Adam and (especially) Eve make a set of wonderful observations about the whole experience. Having heard the voice of the Lord, having been visited and taught by an angel, and having felt the testifying power of the Holy Ghost,

Adam said, "Blessed be the name of God, for because of my transgression my eyes are opened, and in this life *I shall have joy, and again in the flesh I shall see God*" (Moses 5:10; emphasis added; see also Moses 5:4–9).

Adam recognized that agency is a gift from God and that its exercise would both bring joy in this life and ultimately lead him back to God where he wanted to go.

For her part, Eve "heard all these things and was glad, saying: Were it not for our transgression we never should have had seed, and never should have known good and evil, and the joy of our redemption, and the eternal life which God giveth unto all the obedient" (Moses 5:11). It is interesting that Eve, who had already been called "the mother of all living" (Moses 4:26), would make the observation that without the choices they made in the garden "we never should have had seed." Eve recognized that her choice made it possible for the spirit children of our Heavenly Father to come to earth and have physical bodies. Her reverence for creation has been inherited by many of her daughters and is likely the source of the innate spirituality that characterizes many women in the Church still today.

Eve understood that she chose to know "good and evil, and the joy of our redemption, and the eternal life wherein God giveth unto all the obedient" (Moses 5:11). She echoed Adam's expression of joy—"the joy of our redemption." It appears that right from the beginning, our first parents appreciated that they had exercised their gift of agency, had chosen to eat of the tree of the knowledge of good and evil, and chose to experience all the vicissitudes of mortality *in order to have joy!* Lehi clearly understood this concept. As he taught his son Jacob, he authored the insightful and often quoted couplet, "Adam fell that men might be; and men are, that they might have joy" (2 Nephi 2:25).

The Plan of Opposition

Lehi made another important observation concerning agency and the polar opposites represented by such ideas as joy and sorrow or good and evil. He explained, "It must needs be, that there is an opposition in all things. If not so, my first-born in the wilderness, righteousness could not be brought to pass, neither wickedness, neither holiness nor misery, neither good nor bad" (2 Nephi 2:11).

Good and evil define two ends of a spectrum. On one end of the spectrum are evil, wickedness, and misery. On the other end are found goodness, righteousness, and happiness. Lehi continued, explaining that without these defining polar opposites we would "remain as dead, having no life neither death, nor corruption nor incorruption, happiness nor misery, neither sense nor insensibility" (2 Nephi 2:11).

Lehi's view was that existence is defined by the opposites he described and that without them a body would "remain as dead." He elaborated by saying, "Wherefore, it must needs have been created for a thing of naught; wherefore there would have been no purpose in the end of its creation. Wherefore, this thing must needs destroy the wisdom of God and his eternal purposes, and also the power, and the mercy, and the justice of God" (2 Nephi 2:12).

The purpose of creation is to bring to pass righteousness, holiness, goodness, and happiness. For that to happen, there must be opposition or opposite alternatives and choice in all things. Lehi observed that opposition, choice, and agency are essential for existence. Without them there is "no purpose in the end of its creation." Without agency the final result (end of its creation) has no purpose.

Lehi continued by reiterating his point about the relationship between agency and opposition and the eternal purpose of God:

And to bring about his eternal purposes in the end of man, after he had created our first parents, and the beasts of the field and the fowls of the air, and in fine, all things which are created, it must needs be that there was an opposition; even the forbidden fruit in opposition to the tree of life; the one being sweet and the other bitter.

Wherefore, the Lord God gave unto man *that he should act for himself.* Wherefore, *man could not act for himself* save it should be that he was enticed by the one or the other. (2 Nephi 2:15–16; emphasis added)

So that we would understand clearly that his discussion of opposition was in the context of agency and choice, Lehi explained that the "Lord God *gave* unto man that he should *act for himself.*" In other words, Lehi completely understood that agency, or the ability of man to act for himself, was a gift from God. It was given by God to our first parents, who would begin their mortal experience in the Garden of Eden by choosing between the opposites of good and evil.

We know that Adam and Eve were not the only ones to be affected by the exercise of agency in the Garden of Eden. In 1 Corinthians we read that "in Adam all die" (1 Corinthians 15:22). And in Romans is found, "By one man sin entered into the world, and death by sin; and so death passed upon all men" (Romans 5:12). Adam's exercise of agency brought death into the world. We are all subject to death and as such are all affected by the decisions of Adam and Eve.

Those who do not understand the plan of God place the blame for all their ills at the feet of Adam. Were it not for Adam's transgression, as it is spoken of, they assume mankind would still be living in the idyllic garden where there were no cares or troubles of the world. Adam becomes a convenient scapegoat for those to whom agency (decision making) is a burden and not a joy.

A misunderstanding of the nature of Adam's transgression is so pervasive that it is embedded in the theology of major religions. For some, baptism is required to expunge the sin of Adam. This is not sound doctrine, as is pointed out, among other places, in the book of Romans. There we read the following:

> For if by one man's offence death reigned by one; much more they which receive abundance of grace and of the gift of righteousness shall reign in life by one, Jesus Christ.
>
> Therefore as by the offence of one judgment came upon all men to condemnation; even so by the righteousness of one the free gift came upon all men unto justification of life.
>
> For as by one man's disobedience many were made sinners, so by the obedience of one shall many be made righteous. (Romans 5:17–19)

Paul clearly understood that death entered the world through a decision made by one man (Adam). But he also just as clearly understood that through the grace of Christ and His atonement, men would be free from the sin of Adam. The correct doctrine is simply and beautifully articulated in the second article of faith, which states, "We believe that men will be punished for their own sins, and not for Adam's transgression."

Adam and Eve's decision did indeed bring death into the world. But it was part of the plan of God. It is also a part of the plan of God that we would not be held accountable for a decision made by Adam. Adam understood that his exercise of agency had set in motion the plan of God so that men, as Lehi taught, "might have joy." I love Jacob's expression of this same idea. He says,

"Therefore, cheer up your hearts, and remember that ye are free to act for yourselves" (2 Nephi 10:23).

I'm convinced we need to take the scriptures at their word. We need to believe that "men are, that they might have joy" (2 Nephi 2:25). We need to cheer up our hearts. We need to believe that the plan of happiness is aptly named. We need to relish the opportunity to make choices, to exercise our agency, and to recognize that choice is a privilege rather than a burden.

It is not uncommon to feel the burden of choice and yearn for a simpler lifestyle with less pressure and stress. An extreme expression of a simple lifestyle would be the example of life in a monastery. Such a life would be characterized by limited interface with outside influences, few responsibilities, a restricted range of physical and emotional experiences, greatly reduced (if any) family ties, and, as a consequence, seriously reduced choices. No doubt those who choose such a life sincerely believe it will allow them to develop greater spirituality and more piety.

Getting Our Money's Worth

On our bad days we may wish for such an existence. Perhaps in such a life there would be less stress and fewer sorrows. But there would also be fewer joys, fewer ways to serve others, and fewer opportunities to develop the full complement of attributes required to become more like our heavenly parents. We would certainly not be getting our money's worth out of life.

That lingering, gnawing thought—that we need to get our money's worth out of life—was poignantly emphasized in a personal experience some years ago. One of our sons played on a high school basketball team with a young man who one day became so seriously depressed that he took his own life. Our son was asked to speak at the funeral, and I spent some time helping him prepare his talk. I was grateful for the opportunity to be with him and help him work through the feelings he was experiencing in that tender situation. We talked together about his understanding of suicide and discussed how he could express his thoughts to the many other young people who would be attending the funeral. He wanted them to know that what his friend had done was wrong, but wanted at the same time to be sensitive to the tender feelings of family members. It was a tough assignment for a sixteen-year-old boy.

The talk went as well as could be expected, and after the funeral we had another chance to discuss all that had transpired. In that conversation I said something that we both still remember. I was trying to bring closure and put things in terms that a teenager could understand. I expressed the thought that I felt so bad for the boy who took his life because he "didn't get his money's worth."

I have thought about that notion a number of times since then. We all want to get a good deal, to feel like we have gotten full measure for our hard-earned dollars. It seems like life has a way of making sure that we all have plenty of tough experiences to learn from. When that happens, we need to know it's not Adam's fault. Getting a full measure of experience is part of the plan. We should echo the sentiments of Adam, who said, "In this life I shall have joy, and again in the flesh I shall see God" (Moses 5:10).

Thank goodness for the choices of Adam and Eve in the garden. We need to celebrate agency as the wonderful gift from God that it is. Mark Twain was right in one thing—we need to retain all of our liberties and not throw any of them away. We need to exercise agency to experience the joy for which we were created. We need to feel exhilaration for the possibility of obtaining a godlike character and celestial home. We need to go forward with the assurance that our Heavenly Father had supreme confidence in our ability to make His plan work.

Here we are with our agency. Let's make the most of it! Let's get our money's worth!

CHAPTER FOUR

Free Agency or Moral Agency?

I don't care what we do
Where we go, how we get there. . . .
I can do anything I want.
> (The Summer Obsession, "Down for
> Whatever," *This Is Where You Belong*
> [Los Angeles: Virgin Records, 2006],
> audio CD)

THE ATTITUDE ILLUSTRATED by the lyrics of the song, that "I can do anything I want," suggests that the notion of agency may have evolved considerably since being introduced to Adam in the Garden of Eden. Indeed, the term *agency* as used in twenty-first century discourse has come to have multiple meanings or interpretations. For example, consider how the term *free agency* is used in modern professional sports parlance.

A player whose contract has expired is considered to be a *free agent* and can sign a contract offered by another team. Two additional designations are often attached to the term. A professional athlete can be a *restricted free agent,* meaning he or she can sign a new contract but must conform to certain restrictions that generally include compensation paid to the former team. *Unrestricted free agents* have no limitations on their agency and are free to sign any contracts offered to them. Unrestricted free agency, or the idea expressed in the song that "I can do anything I want," is for some the new definition of agency.

It is not clear how or when the combination of the words *free* or *freedom* and *agency* became associated with the notion of unbounded liberty. What is clear is that unbounded and unfettered liberty is thought of as an entitlement in today's society. "I have the right to do whatever I want" is the common mantra heard among people of all ages. It is an especially appealing idea to teenagers who are testing the boundaries that have been suggested by parents. But unfettered rights are not the sole purview of teenagers. Adults use the same phrase to justify all sorts of behavior. The most hotly debated issues in our society concern individual "rights." Among these debated rights are the right to an abortion, the right to view pornography, and the right to sexual experiences between consenting adults regardless of sexual orientation.

Those who clamor for the completely unbounded agency of the individual are not likely to be dissuaded from their position by an examination of what God meant by agency. Nevertheless, thoughtful people of every religious persuasion—and especially Latter-day Saints—should try to have a more complete understanding of God's view of agency. That understanding comes best from a careful reading of the scriptures and the statements of modern prophets and apostles.

We have discussed that the first exercise of agency for the first mortal man, Adam, and first mortal woman, Eve, was the choice of whether or not to partake of the fruit of the tree of the knowledge of good and evil. It was clear from the beginning that God's focus was on our knowing good from evil. Indeed, it was the knowledge of good and evil that was to make men and women gods. This important point was known even to the devil: "And the serpent said unto the woman, Ye shall not surely die: For God doth know that in the day ye eat thereof, then your eyes shall be opened, and ye shall be *as gods, knowing good and evil*" (Genesis 3:4–5; emphasis added). This point is further underscored in a conversation between the Father and His Son that is found in the book of Moses: "And I, the Lord God, said unto mine Only Begotten: Behold, the man *is become as one of us to know good and evil*" (Moses 4:28; emphasis added). Lehi, in his teaching to his son Jacob, states, "Men are instructed sufficiently that *they know good from evil*" (2 Nephi 2:5; emphasis added).

Alma observes, "Wherefore, he gave commandments unto men, they having first transgressed the first commandments as to things which were temporal, and *becoming as Gods, knowing good from evil,* placing themselves in a state to act, or being placed in a state to act according to their wills and pleasures, *whether to do evil or to do good*" (Alma 12:31; emphasis added).

God's intent, His plan, if you will, was and is that man become as He is. Becoming as gods requires *both* that man have a knowledge of good and evil *and* that men and women be placed "in a state to act according to their wills and pleasures, whether to do evil or to do good." In other words, God intended, first, that we learn the difference between good and evil and, second, that we learn to act on that difference by either doing good or doing evil.

This is the classic definition of morality (knowing the difference between good and evil) and of moral behavior (choosing between good and evil or right and wrong). Thus, the agency that

God gave as a gift is *moral agency,* the right to choose between good and evil, right and wrong, and through our choices become *as gods.*

President Boyd K. Packer made a clear distinction between free agency and moral agency in his April 1992 conference talk. He said: "The phrase 'free agency' does not appear in scripture. The only agency spoken of there is *moral agency* which, the Lord said, 'I have given unto him, that every man might be accountable for his own sins in the day of judgment' (D&C 101:78)" (in Conference Report, April 1992, 92; emphasis added).

Nevertheless, on several occasions in the scriptures the term *free* is found in a discussion of agency-related concepts. For example, Lehi says, "And because that they are redeemed from the fall *they have become free forever,* knowing good from evil; to act for themselves and not to be acted upon" (2 Nephi 2:26). He goes on to say, "Wherefore, men are *free* according to the flesh. . . . And they are *free to choose* liberty and eternal life, through the great Mediator of all men, or to choose captivity and death, according to the captivity and power of the devil" (2 Nephi 2:27; emphasis added).

Lehi makes it clear what he means by free when he says, "free to choose liberty and eternal life . . . or to choose captivity and death." The freedom of choice for Lehi is clearly in the context of choosing between good, liberty, and eternal life, and evil, captivity, and death. Lehi's freedom is the freedom of moral choice, *not* a freedom to do whatever one wants. Lehi also makes it clear that freedom of choice involves the consequences of liberty and eternal life or captivity and death.

Jacob uses the word *free* in exactly the same manner when he says, "Therefore, cheer up your hearts, and remember that *ye are free* to act for yourselves—to choose the way of everlasting death or the way of eternal life" (2 Nephi 10:23; emphasis added). Jacob says in essence you are free to choose between evil ("the way of everlasting death") or good ("the way of eternal life"). Jacob may well have said, Cheer up your hearts; you have the *privilege* of choice, the *privilege* to act for yourself.

The clearest expression of the link between the word *free* and the scriptural concept of agency is found in the teaching of the prophet Samuel the Lamanite: "Whosoever doeth iniquity, doeth it unto himself; for behold, *ye are free;* ye are permitted to act for yourselves; for behold, God hath given unto you a knowledge and *he hath made you free. He hath given unto you that ye might know good from evil,* and he hath given unto you that ye might choose life or death" (Helaman 14:30–31; emphasis added). Samuel clearly equates being made free with having a knowledge of good and evil. To be free is not to be unbounded. To be free is the opportunity to exercise the choice between good and evil. To be free is to have a knowledge of the consequences of our actions. To be free refers to the opportunity to exercise moral agency and not be forced to do either right or wrong. As we will see, we do not have unbounded freedom, nor are we free from the consequences of acting as if we did.

The Paradox of "Free Agency"

It seems that few appreciate the paradox inherent in the use of the term *free agency.* The freedom of choice that we exercise here in this mortal state is anything but free. It came at an enormous price, just as freedom from totalitarian rule required two world wars and some of the best blood of the twentieth century. The Apostle Paul made this point to the Corinthians when he said, "What? know ye not that your body is the temple of the Holy Ghost which is in you, which ye have of God, and ye are not your own? For ye are bought with a price" (1 Corinthians 6:19–20). The price for the Father's plan—and the agency that is so essential to it—was paid by the spilt blood of Christ as He suffered in

Gethsemane and on Calvary. Without His atoning sacrifice we could not in any way be free.

Lehi eloquently teaches this concept to his son Jacob in the following words:

> The Messiah cometh in the fulness of time, that he may redeem the children of men from the fall. *And because that they are redeemed from the fall they have become free forever,* knowing good from evil; to act for themselves and not to be acted upon, save it be by the punishment of the law at the great and last day, according to the commandments which God hath given. (2 Nephi 2:26; emphasis added)

It is the atoning sacrifice of Christ that redeemed men from the fall and makes them *"free forever, knowing good from evil."* Lehi understood that the freedom purchased by the atonement was freedom to make moral choices or to know good from evil. He clearly makes the point that moral agency is not to be considered as unbridled freedom to do whatever one wishes. The point is made by stating that "they . . . become free forever, . . . to act for themselves and not to be acted upon, *save it be by the punishment of the law* at the great and last day."

Actions have consequences. The freedom to choose is not freedom from consequences. Punishment must accompany a broken law.

As noted earlier, the truth that in the economy of a just God there would have to be punishment for broken laws was well understood in the premortal existence. Without the provision of an atoning sacrifice, the Father's gift of agency would have had far fewer takers. Yes, some intrepid souls may have believed that they would always make correct choices and thereby avoid serious punishments. And others may even have believed they could survive severe punishments and gain the eventual rewards.

But the promise of a savior, a redeemer who would suffer vicariously for our sins (which offering we could partake of when we come unto Christ and repent), surely made it possible for many more, who would have faith in that redeemer, to choose the Father's plan and accept the responsibility and reward of moral agency that accompanied the plan. It is only because Christ was willing to suffer in incalculable ways that we have agency. The gift of agency given by the Father was paid for by the Son. The gift was given in conjunction with a savior so we might not fear the process of gaining wisdom and judgment through our own experiences. The gift is abused when we consider agency to be unbridled freedom for self-indulgence. Those who do not understand the true nature of agency, who do not avail themselves of the atonement through a broken heart and contrite spirit of repentance, will ultimately have to suffer for their own sins. These would have wished for a better understanding of the relationship of agency and the atonement of Jesus Christ.

There is another sense in which the term *free agency* is a paradox. This concept is insignificant when compared to the price paid by the Savior of the world; nevertheless, it is worth considering. In a way, we each individually pay a price through the anxiety, trauma, and emotional upset we experience because of things we can't explain. When faced with uncertainty, injustice, and unanswered questions, we suffer. A latter-day apostle, Elder Richard L. Evans, observed:

> Some of the ponderable problems, the unanswered questions, the seeming injustices and discrepancies and uncertainties . . . which we often have a difficult time in reconciling, will find answer and solution and satisfaction

if we are patient and prayerful and willing to wait. Part of them are the price we pay for our free agency. We pay a great price for free agency in this world, but it is worth the price we pay. One of the cherished sentences I recall from the utterances of the prophet Joseph Smith is the one which says that "an hour of virtuous liberty on earth is worth a whole eternity of bondage." So long as men have their free agency, there will be temporary injustices and discrepancies and some seemingly inexplicable things, which ultimately in our Father's own time and purpose will be reconciled and made right. (Conference Report, April 1952, 67–68)

Perhaps the emotional price we pay is proportional to our lack of understanding. The less we understand about agency, the more anguish and the higher price we pay. The more we understand about agency and about the Savior's atonement, the more we are willing to let the price He has already paid reduce the price we pay. The Savior's atonement is meant not only to pay the price for the mistakes we make, but also to comfort us because of the mistakes of others.

This important purpose of the Savior's atonement, to provide comfort and solace to the Father's children, is explained beautifully by Tad R. Callister:

One of the blessings of the atonement is that we can receive of the Savior's succoring powers. Isaiah spoke repeatedly of the Lord's healing calming influence. He testified that the Savior was "a strength to the needy in his distress, a refuge from the storm, a shadow from the heat" (Isaiah 25:4). As to those who sorrow, Isaiah declared that the Savior possessed the power to "comfort all that mourn"

(Isaiah 61:2), and "wipe away tears from off all faces" (Isaiah 25:8; see also Revelation 7:17); "revive the spirit of the humble" (Isaiah 57:15); and "bind up the broken-hearted" (Isaiah 61:1; see also Luke 4:18; Psalm 147:3). So expansive was his succoring power that he could exchange "beauty for ashes, the oil of joy for mourning, the garment of praise for the spirit of heaviness" (Isaiah 61:3). (*The Infinite Atonement* [Salt Lake City: Deseret Book, 2000], 206)

The emotional price we pay for agency can be reduced by the Savior's atonement. In addition to paying for our sins, His atoning sacrifice gives Him the power to comfort us in every way described by Isaiah and more. How grateful we should be to the Savior for paying the price for "free" agency.

Moral Agency and Wisdom

Let us return for a moment to the experience of Eve in the Garden of Eden. Eve explained to the serpent that she and Adam had been commanded not to eat of the fruit of the tree of the knowledge of good and evil. His reply was that if she did eat of the fruit her eyes would be open and she would become as God, knowing good and evil. The scriptures then recount, "And when the woman saw that the tree was good for food, and that it became pleasant to the eyes, *and a tree to be desired to make her wise,* she took of the fruit thereof" (Moses 4:12; emphasis added). Implied in that passage is the concept that knowing good and evil is the essence of wisdom.

In other words, the wisdom that God is most interested in having us obtain is *moral wisdom*. Undoubtedly, we are to become wise in all aspects of life; but above all we are to become wise in knowing right from wrong.

Consider in this context the enormous difference in secular knowledge and wisdom between those living in any past century and those who live in the twenty-first century. If success in navigating this life were based on secular wisdom, those living in our day would, in the vernacular, have it made! While secular wisdom may be dependent on the historic era in which one lives, moral wisdom is not. The wisdom of knowing right from wrong is a standard against which men of all ages can be judged.

The view that wisdom is knowing good from evil is not the definition of wisdom found in a modern dictionary. Let us briefly consider the dictionary definition of wisdom.

The Merriam Webster on-line dictionary has *good sense* and *judgment* as synonyms for wisdom. It further indicates that *wisdom* implies *sense and judgment far above average. Sense,* the dictionary says, implies a reliable ability to judge and decide with soundness, prudence, and intelligence. *Judgment* implies sense tempered and refined by experience, training, and maturity. Combining these terms yields a definition of wisdom: Far above average ability to judge and decide with soundness, prudence, and intelligence, tempered and refined by experience, training, and maturity.

This is a good definition of secular wisdom which, when extended, can be helpful in our understanding of how we are to become wise in this mortal experience. But now let's add the words "between good and evil" to this definition to give us a Garden of Eden notion of wisdom. Wisdom then becomes "A far above average ability to judge and decide between good and evil."

The wisdom we seek is *moral wisdom,* born from the exercise of moral agency. Judging between good and evil with "soundness, prudence, and intelligence" suggests that the process is rational and can be reproduced. "Tempered and refined by experience, training, and maturity" is a good description of what happens from childhood to old age. We are trained and taught good from evil, hopefully by loving parents. We have experiences during which we exercise agency by practicing what we have been trained to do. Over time, we mature in our ability to discern and judge between good and evil in all its manifestations and thus to become wise.

Clearly, becoming wise requires that we exercise the God-given gift of moral agency. Each step in the process of weighing alternatives, identifying consequences, applying judgment, and gaining perspective from past experience would be meaningless in the absence of agency. God intends that our exercise of agency will render us wise in every possible way, but His number-one objective for us is that we exercise moral agency to gain moral wisdom.

Our Heavenly Father's great desire is that we learn to distinguish good from evil in our earthly experience. We receive no heavenly pronouncements concerning correct principles in politics, economics, science, or any of the other human pursuits except insofar as they are affected by the universal issues of right and wrong.

Essentially, it is the exercise of moral agency that results in the moral wisdom God intended His children to acquire. It is not the choice between a red bicycle and a blue one or between a Ford and Chevrolet that concerns our Heavenly Father. The moral choices—those that have eternal consequences and determine whether or not we return to His presence—are those toward which He particularly wishes the gift of agency be applied.

Helps for Parents and Priesthood Leaders

I believe there is a major payoff to priesthood leaders and parents who teach these concepts to their children. Parents should take to heart the counsel of President Boyd K. Packer, who said, "The study of the doctrines of the gospel will improve behavior quicker than talking about behavior will improve behavior" ("Washed Clean," *Ensign,* May 1997, 9). Teaching the gospel doctrine of *moral agency* is an excellent example of the principle espoused by President Packer.

The teaching could be done in four parts. Part one would be a discussion of the distinction between moral agency and free agency. Scriptures cited in this chapter could be read and discussed so that children and teenagers know that their Heavenly Father really cares that they know right from wrong. When asked, they would undoubtedly be able to provide examples of the "I can do anything I want" notion of unbridled "free" agency and the entitlement mentality it fosters. The object of the part one discussion is to help youth clearly make the doctrinal distinction between moral agency and their previously held notion of free agency.

Part two of the teaching would be a discussion of the concept of wisdom and the difference between secular wisdom and moral wisdom. Most children want very much to be thought of as wise. It is helpful to them to be taught exactly what it means to be wise and what things it is most important to be wise about. Parents and children together could study the definition of wisdom and share with each other the myriad examples that are found in the scriptures and everyday experiences.

Part three would focus on the concept that agency is not free. Children can be taught that their ability to make choices is a gift from a loving Heavenly Father and that the gift was paid for by the suffering of His Son. They will understand that when they give a birthday present to a friend, the present or gift was paid for by someone—either themselves or their parents. They can be taught that agency is a gift of great value, and therefore it should be used wisely and well.

Part four of the teaching could focus on the important concept of consequences. The key notion is that actions have consequences, and while we are free to choose an action we are not free to choose the consequences that accompany that action. As mentioned, children want to be wise. They can be taught that people who are wise understand that actions have consequences and people who are foolish tend to ignore that important fact.

I am convinced that these important principles can be taught to children and that when they better understand moral agency they will be more wise in their decision making. The immediate benefits to both children and parents should be clear. More important, the long-term benefit is that we, with our children, experience God's intent for us as He verbalized it to His Son: "And I, the Lord God, said unto mine Only Begotten: Behold, the man is become as one of us to know good and evil" (Moses 4:28).

CHAPTER FIVE

Agency and Consequences

THE GREAT MISCONCEPTION of "free" agency is that one can have the privilege of choice and somehow avoid the responsibility of consequences. Someone has said that a Statue of Responsibility should be erected on the west coast to balance the Statue of Liberty that stands on the east coast. Young people, especially, have an asymmetric view of agency; they tend to focus on the positive outcomes they associate with making their own choices and ignore the potential negative outcomes. The following story, written by radio talk-show host Bob Lonsberry, is one of thousands that could be used to illustrate the principle of agency and consequences.

This is the story of John and some choices he made.
It ends beneath an underpass with the Bishop hanging upside down, crumpled inside what remained of the family car. There had just been a hellacious collision and the

Jetta came to a rest ripped to smithereens, a jumble of broken glass and twisted metal.

In pain, the Bishop thought first of his family, and looking around discovered what had been done in an instant.

His wife, pregnant with a baby boy, sitting beside him in the front seat, was dead. His 11-year-old son was dead in the back seat and so was his 9-year-old daughter. His 6-year-old son was alive but had suffered a major brain injury.

That's where it ended.

It began at John's house. . . .

He is 17, with three years on the varsity football team, an Eagle Scout, seminary student, and an active member of his Priests' Quorum. He is a Mormon kid growing up like so many other Mormon kids in Utah.

He has had the advantage of a loving, gospel-centered home, and a ward, school and community support system designed to give him every opportunity to grow into a righteous and useful man.

Like so many LDS youth, he had the benefit of being taught the gospel and the importance of faith in Jesus Christ. He has been instructed countless times about the commandments the Lord has given to protect and bless his life.

And still, police say, he was behind the wheel of a speeding truck, in the wrong lane, roaring head-on against traffic, with almost twice the legal limit of alcohol in his bloodstream. As the Bishop swerved to get out of the way, witnesses said John swerved as well, directly into the Jetta.

That's how he became a killer.

John, a senior in high school, crawled out of the

wreckage of his truck and ran several blocks before police caught up with him. When ordered to take a field sobriety test, police said, he responded that he couldn't, that he was too drunk. . . .

This is the story of John and some choices he made.

This is the story of an LDS kid who memorized the Articles of Faith, sang in the Primary presentations, had family prayer and grew up in a good Mormon home. This is the story of an LDS kid a lot like you.

A kid who heard but did not do, promised but did not fulfill, professed but did not practice. A kid who did not understand what a commandment is.

It is a protection, not a punishment; a shield, not a chain. It is a warning from a loving heavenly parent. The Lord gives us commandments not to make us miserable, or to deprive us of enjoyments, but to keep us out of trouble, to spare us the miseries and sufferings that are eventually and unavoidably tied to unrighteous conduct.

Commandments are not given for God's benefit, but for ours. They are rules of safety, akin to a parent telling a child not to stick things in a light socket.

But John didn't listen.

Not that night behind the wheel. And see what has come. Think about what happened.

Imagine what has been lost. List the victims, contemplate the emotions, and count the cost.

And think about yourself.

Think about the consequences of your own choices. Are they apt to be joy and peace, or pain and suffering? Do they have the potential to be devastatingly wrong? Could they leave blood on your hands? If not the blood of an innocent family, then of an innocent Lord who was crucified for us and because of us. . . . *This is a lesson in the power of personal choice,* and the importance of a righteous choice.

This is the story of John.

But it's really about you.

And what you decide your story will be. (Bob Lonsberry, "A Story for Mormon Teens," http://www .Lonsberry.com/writings.cfm?story=2090&go=4; names have been changed; emphasis added; used by permission)

What a sad but illuminating story about agency and consequences. Unfortunately, it is only one of many that could be told. One result of casually blurring the concept of *moral* agency with *free* agency is the implication that unfettered choice is also somehow *free from consequence.* It is doubtlessly pleasing to the devil, who seeks to make "all men miserable like unto himself" (2 Nephi 2:27), that the relationship between choice and accountability is constantly being obscured. Misery is definitely the result of making choices without regard to the consequences that may follow.

A little experience teaches that while a person may indeed be free to choose an action, he or she is not free to choose the consequences that accompany the action.

Our understanding of consequences increases dramatically with age and experience. We may be told that a given choice or act has a particular consequence, but until the consequence is experienced personally, the discussion is mostly academic or conceptual. Learning a principle from our own experience in life's laboratory is more powerful than any conceptual discussion of that principle. One of the great challenges of life is to learn about choices and outcomes from those experiences that are less serious instead of more serious. Hopefully we learn about the consequences of gravity by jumping off the couch before we try jumping off the roof.

We can learn about fire by touching it with our hand before we allow it to burn our whole body.

Parents have the major responsibility to monitor and maintain a balance in the learning process. They cannot constantly shield their children from the consequences of their actions in the ill-conceived notion that such a practice is good parenting. Using money, influence, or other means to protect children from experiencing the link between actions and consequences often leads to disastrous outcomes. Children so treated usually end up with very poor judgment and ultimately make serious errors that cannot be mitigated by parents. In such cases, society has to step in and impose sanctions and penalties that are much more severe than would have been the case if the individual had been allowed at an earlier date to personally experience the link between agency and consequences.

On the other hand, the desired balance in the learning process can be undone by parents who push their children too fast into certain kinds of experiences. Children can be encouraged by well-meaning parents into all kinds of activities before they are prepared for the consequences. A certain level of maturity and judgment is needed before a boy is given a gun to shoot, a four-wheeler or jet ski to drive, an axe to wield, or a motorcycle to ride. Girls who are encouraged as preteens into provocative dress and behavior are poorly prepared for the potential consequences of such actions.

Parents' good judgment in their own behavior can do much to help children learn about consequences. Driving when drinking, speeding, scoffing at the law, credit card debt, physical abuse, dishonesty, and a host of other parental behaviors can send messages to children that such behaviors have little or no earthly consequences. Parents need to "walk the walk" if they expect to fulfill their responsibility in teaching about agency and consequences.

Parents can also "talk the talk" about consequences. The family dinner table is an excellent setting for discussions about good decisions and bad decisions. Examples can be used from newspaper reports, neighborhood events, family activities, and scriptural accounts, among others. Family home evenings, family councils, and one-on-one activities with children also provide excellent settings for discussing actions and consequences. Some children can learn on their own from observation; most need parents who involve children in discussions (not lectures) so that the children benefit from the thought processes and judgment of mature adults who have more experience than they have.

An important element in the discussion of consequences is the differentiation between earthly consequences and heavenly or eternal consequences. Some important major differences exist between the laws of God and the laws of man and the consequences that follow the breaking of each.

In the first place, men's laws are finite, and the breaking of those laws results in finite consequences. However, God's laws are eternal and have eternal consequences. In the second place, the laws of society are less and less patterned after the laws of God. For example, the laws of God concerning chastity and moral purity are quite clear, and we are constantly counseled about the eternal consequences of breaking those laws. By contrast, most Western societies have long since given up on trying to punish any kind of immoral conduct. This creates a serious problem for parents who wish to teach eternal truths and eternal consequences. When our youth observe immoral behavior in television shows, movies, lyrics of songs they listen to, and even among their peers, and they observe that that behavior seems to have little or no consequence, it becomes imperative that parents emphasize the truths inherent in the laws of God.

For more than two decades the young women of the Church

around the world have been standing and reciting together the Young Women theme, which in part says, "we will stand as 'witnesses of God at all times and in all things, and in all places' (Mosiah 18:9) as we strive to live the Young Women values, which are: faith, divine nature, individual worth, knowledge, *choice and accountability*, good works, and integrity" (emphasis added). The theme appropriately focuses attention on *standing as witnesses of God.* The values espoused are values of God, not values of man. *Choice and accountability* is a true principle that will be enforced by God regardless of the laws of man.

The principles of agency and accountability are spelled out beautifully in the *For the Strength of Youth* pamphlet published by the Church. Page four of the pamphlet, under the heading of "Agency and Accountability," quotes the scripture, "Wherefore, men . . . are free to choose liberty and eternal life, through the great Mediator of all men, or to choose captivity and death" (2 Nephi 2:27). After the scripture are found the following paragraphs:

> Your Heavenly Father has given you agency, the ability to choose right from wrong and to act for yourself. You have been given the Holy Ghost to help you know good from evil. While you are here on earth, you are being proven to see if you will use your agency to show your love for God by keeping His commandments.
>
> While you are free to choose for yourself, you are not free to choose the consequences of your actions. When you make a choice, you will receive the consequences of that choice. The consequences may not be immediate, but they will always follow, for good or bad. Wrong choices delay your progression and lead to heartache and misery. Right choices lead to happiness and eternal life. That is why it is

so important for you to choose what is right throughout your life.

You are responsible for the choices you make. You should not blame your circumstances, your family, or your friends if you choose to disobey God's commandments. You are a child of God with great strength. You have the ability to choose righteousness and happiness, no matter what your circumstances. (*For the Strength of Youth: Fulfilling Our Duty to God* [Salt Lake City: The Church of Jesus Christ of Latter-day Saints, 2001], 4–5)

The counsel in these paragraphs is given lovingly and with the great hope that it will be followed. It is given by men and women in the highest Church leadership positions, who have firm testimonies of the value of eternal principles. It is given to our youth with the sure knowledge that eternal blessings await those young people who exercise their agency in accordance with eternal principles instead of the precepts of men.

One of the often ignored consequences of agency is that good choices lead to more choices and poor choices lead to fewer choices. Indeed, a paradox of our modern society, which places so much emphasis on unbridled free agency, is that the exercise of unbridled—*I can do anything I want*—agency leads ultimately not to more freedom and more choices but to less freedom and fewer choices.

Unbridled choice sooner or later leads to law breaking, which results, depending on severity and frequency, in a succession of circumstances involving less and less freedom. First might come probation, involving loss of privileges and some restricted freedom. Next might come a detention center for youth or an arrangement of days at work and nights in jail for adults. Severe abusers of the law are found in prison, and within prison some are placed in solitary confinement, which involves a total loss of freedom and choice.

Lehi attempted to teach this important principle to his sons. He observed:

> And the Messiah cometh in the fullness of time, that he may redeem the children of men from the fall. And because that they are redeemed from the fall they have become free forever, knowing good from evil; to act for themselves and not to be acted upon, *save it be by the punishment of the law* at the great and last day, according to the commandments which God hath given.
>
> Wherefore, men are free according to the flesh; and all things are given them which are expedient unto man. And they are free to choose liberty and eternal life, through the great Mediator of all men, or to choose captivity and death, according to the captivity and power of the devil; for he seeketh that all men might be miserable like unto himself. (2 Nephi 2:26–27; emphasis added)

Lehi explains that because of the mediation, or atonement, of Christ, individuals in mortality are free to choose "to act for themselves and not to be acted upon, *save it be by the punishment of the law.*" In other words, men can act for themselves and not be acted upon *until a law is broken.* At that point, some form of punishment is given as the consequence of the broken law. The punishment both on earth and in heaven inevitably involves a restriction of freedom and future choice. On earth, punishment is often captivity in prison. In heaven, the ultimate punishment will be "captivity and death, according to the captivity and power of the devil."

It is significant that after mortality those who have broken God's laws and have not repented find themselves in a place called spirit prison. This term aptly describes the reduced freedom and restricted choices that must be endured as consequences of poor choices made on earth.

How important it is for young people to be taught that good choices lead to more choices and bad choices lead to fewer choices!

What happens if, in spite of being well taught and having good intentions, we make poor choices? Fortunately, there is a provision in the plan for just such an eventuality.

As previously noted, we knew full well in our premortal life that God is a God of justice. We knew that the laws of God could be followed with attendant good outcomes (blessings) or bad outcomes (punishments) and that we could count on both being administered fairly. Satan's themes were fear and punishment. The Savior spoke about faith and blessings. We ultimately came to earth because we sought the blessings and because we were taught about "agency and how to recover from it." The need for a recovery mechanism was clearly understood by our Heavenly Father and was explicitly built into the plan under which we agreed to go forward into a second estate. Making the decision to be involved in the plan was apparently not an easy one. We are aware that one-third of the hosts of heaven did not wish to participate and exercised their agency by choosing to not be included in the plan.

One reason for the decision could very well have been the fear that the recovery provisions in the plan would not work. Some may have feared that in the exercise of their agency they would make many errors in judgment and that the consequences of those judgment errors would lead to outcomes they were unwilling to experience.

Another word for recovery is *salvage*. In this context let me recount a tender and true story about the teaching of the gospel to a family in Switzerland. Our missionaries in Geneva had contacted a family from Romania who seemed interested in hearing more about the message of the gospel. The family consisted of a father, mother, and three boys, ages sixteen, twelve, and ten. The father and mother spoke no French or English, the oldest boy spoke some English, and the two youngest spoke a little French. The missionaries taught the family by speaking to the oldest boy in English and having him translate into Romanian for the rest of the family.

On one occasion I went with the missionaries to teach the family, and I was pleased to see that the process seemed to be working, although it was slow and required frequent repeating and reviewing. After some months, when the family had all read the Book of Mormon in Romanian and had attended church a number of times, the missionaries were convinced that all five members of the family were ready for baptism. A baptismal interview was scheduled, and interviews were conducted with each family member. During the interview with the father, the missionary zone leader doing the interview sensed that the father still had a few questions and so spent some time in additional teaching and clarifying. At the end of the interview the zone leader asked if the father would like to kneel and pray one more time in order to be assured he was making the right decision.

The father and missionary knelt together, and the father began to pray in Romanian. The missionary recounted to me that as the father began his prayer the missionary heard the increasingly intrusive sound of an ambulance siren somewhere not far distant. He said, "President, I was worried that the siren would be a distraction so I began to pray that the siren would quit. It didn't quit but got louder and louder, and I got more and more anxious and prayed harder and harder." At almost the same instant the father ended his prayer, the sound of the ambulance siren also ceased. The man rose from his knees, turned to the missionary, and said he was now ready to be baptized. He then said in broken French and English,

"Oh, by the way, did you know that in Romanian the word for 'ambulance' is the same word as the word for 'salvation'?"

We attended the baptismal service for the entire family. The father and mother were baptized first. Their baptisms were performed by one of the missionaries who had met and taught them. The baptismal prayer was pronounced in Romanian, which the missionary had learned, practiced, and memorized. The oldest boy was baptized in English by another missionary. The two youngest boys were baptized by a member who had been instrumental in fellowshipping the family, and the prayer was pronounced in French.

Agency sometimes requires a major salvage operation. The gospel ambulance can carry each of us to the atonement, where, through sincere repentance, we can be healed and recover from the consequences of our actions. But the salvage process takes time, effort, and dedication, and it is much more difficult than if we had done it right to begin with. This is intended to teach us to make better use of our agency in the future. But, make no mistake, the process works. The Savior's atoning sacrifice was made precisely so that we can exercise agency and learn from experience without forfeiting our eternal inheritance. The poor choices we make in breaking God's laws, which would otherwise result in eternal (God's) punishments (see D&C 19:11), can be avoided through the repentance process. The Savior promised that those who sincerely repent would be forgiven and He would suffer their punishment for them.

The atonement is the second great gift our Father has given us, but second only in chronology. In every other measurable way it is unquestionably the greatest gift. Without an atonement that is infinite in time, place, and manner, one could conceive that there could be a time (past, present, or future), or a place (on this world or other worlds), or a manner of sin that would be beyond the reach of the Savior's atoning sacrifice. One could then conceive such severe consequences flowing from that circumstance that the gift of agency would be rejected. Agency in such a setting would be as fearful as the devil attempted to portray it.

But the infinite atonement was part of the plan. Indeed, it was the centerpiece of the plan presented in the premortal existence. As previously noted, the war in heaven over conflicting plans was won by focusing on the atonement. Testimony was provided that it was the divine mechanism by which the Father's children could overcome the negative consequences of agency and realize its blessings.

In sum, we know that agency is not "free" and that actions have consequences. We should be grateful every day for the love of the Father and the Son and the two great gifts they have given us: the gift of agency, given that we might make choices that will lead us back to the Father; and the incomparable gift of the atonement, which allows us to recover from consequences, be comforted in the process, and, in the end, be sanctified and reunited with the Father.

CHAPTER SIX

Political Agency

We the people of the United States, in order to form a more perfect Union, establish justice, insure domestic tranquility, provide for the common defense, promote the general welfare, and *secure the blessings of liberty* to ourselves and our posterity, do ordain and establish this Constitution for the United States of America. (Preamble, United States Constitution; emphasis added)

THE PREAMBLE TO THE United States Constitution is familiar to many Americans. Clearly, securing the blessings of liberty or agency and choice was of major importance to the framers of the Constitution. The founding fathers were greatly disturbed by the abuses they had experienced under English rule on the new American continent, and their aim was to establish a document that would preserve the rights of the people. The desired rights included, among others, freedom of religion, speech, press, petition, and assembly; the right to bear arms; freedom from unlawful search and seizure; the right to due process of the law; trial by jury; and freedom from cruel and unusual punishment. These rights, enumerated in the Bill of Rights, comprise the first ten amendments to the United States Constitution. They describe the freedoms that have made the United States a beacon of liberty for people around the world. In a broad sense, a democracy that secures the individual freedoms of its citizens could be construed to be the political embodiment of the God-given gift of agency.

The Constitution of the United States has been the foundation for a democracy that has existed for more than two hundred years. Despite some very notable exceptions, individual agency has fared reasonably well under the United States Constitution. But two hundred years is *not* a very long time in the history of the agency God has given to man. Throughout that history, a wide variety of political systems have been employed to rule society. In addition to democracy, those systems include aristocracy, autocracy, anarchy, despotism, dictatorship, monarchy, oligarchy, and numerous others. Of course, some have been more successful than others, as judged by the productivity, culture, and creativity of their citizens.

It has been established from the scriptures that the kind of agency God gave to Adam and his posterity is moral agency, or the opportunity to know good and evil and choose between right and wrong. The descendants of Adam through the ages have lived under every kind of political arrangement, including all of those mentioned above. We may ask, is it only those people who have lived under democratic rule who have been able to truly exercise moral agency? Is it only in a democracy that individuals can gain the benefits that God intended from our sojourn on earth?

First-Order Moral Agency

The answer is that the exercise of the moral agency given to man is independent of the political system in which one lives. To support that statement, I would like to define something I will call *first-order moral agency.* Let us define first-order moral agency as choosing between right and wrong (good and evil) *in the behavior of one individual toward another.* Included in that definition would be actions of an individual toward family, friends, and neighbors. Of course, the two individuals need not be related, as suggested by the Savior's parable of the good Samaritan.

When we look at the Ten Commandments in connection with first-order moral behavior, we see how much choice one can have regardless of the political system he lives under. To put the issue in context, consider an experience of Moses:

> And it came to pass on the morrow, that Moses sat to judge the people: and the people stood by Moses from the morning unto the evening.
>
> And when Moses' father in law saw all that he did to the people, he said, What is this thing that thou doest to the people? why sittest thou thyself alone, and all the people stand by thee from morning unto even?
>
> And Moses said unto his father in law, Because the people come unto me to enquire of God:
>
> When they have a matter, they come unto me; and I judge between one and another, and I do make them know the statures of God, and his laws.
>
> And Moses' father in law said unto him, The thing that thou doest is not good.
>
> Thou wilt surely wear away, both thou, and this people that is with thee: for this thing is too heavy for thee; thou are not able to perform it thyself alone.

Hearken now unto my voice, I will give thee counsel,
and God shall be with thee: Be thou for the people to
God-ward, that thou mayest bring the causes unto God:

And thou shalt teach them ordinances and laws, and
shalt shew them the way wherein they must walk, and the
work that they must do. (Exodus 18:13–20)

The children of Egypt, after being brought out of captivity,
needed guidance on how to live. Moses was providing that guidance in one-on-one encounters, but his father-in-law observed that
that approach was good neither for Moses nor for the people. His
counsel to Moses was that he should continue to stand as God's
representative before the people—to continue to present their cases
before God. But he was also to teach the people the ordinances
and laws of God and have them begin to exercise individual moral
agency. He was to teach correct principles and let the people begin
what would be the long and slow process of learning to make correct choices without being told what to do by their masters or by
Moses.

It is in this context that Moses went up on Mount Sinai and
received the Ten Commandments that would provide direct teaching from God as to what was right and wrong. The first four commandments are "Thou shalt have no other Gods before me. Thou
shalt not make unto thee any graven image. . . . Thou shalt not
take the name of the Lord thy God in vain. . . . Remember the
sabbath day, to keep it holy" (Exodus 20: 3–4, 7–8). These commandments deal with the correct behavior of one individual
toward another individual—but not just any other individual.
They set out the difference between good and evil as it pertains
to the relationship between a person and God. It would be evil to
worship someone other than God; to make or worship idols;
to swear, make an oath, or in any other fashion take the name of

God in vain; or to forget God on His one day of the week. These laws detailing the correct relationship with God clearly fit into the definition of first-order moral agency.

The next six commandments are "Honour thy father and thy mother. . . . Thou shalt not kill. . . . Thou shalt not commit adultery. . . . Thou shalt not steal. Thou shalt not bear false witness against thy neighbour. . . . Thou shalt not covet thy neighbour's house, thou shalt not covet thy neighbour's wife, nor his manservant, nor his maidservant, nor his ox, nor his ass, nor anything that is thy neighbour's" (Exodus 20:12–17). Obviously these last six commandments deal very directly with the good and evil behavior of one individual toward another.

The point is that individuals can and must exercise first-order moral agency regardless of the political system in which they find themselves. A given political system may provide more or less personal liberty or agency, but the nature of the political system does not abrogate the responsibility that individuals have to exercise what has been defined as first-order moral agency. In other words, whether an individual lives in a dictatorship, democracy, or anarchy he or she can learn to know good from evil and thus fulfill one of the purposes of God's plan. It was not the intention of God that the Ten Commandments be valid only in a few special political arrangements.

An extreme example will make the point. Some have experienced a complete lack of personal freedom through the deprivation and cruelty of prisons and concentration camps and still maintained their moral compass. One such example is found in Viktor E. Frankl's account of his experience in a Nazi concentration camp. He says:

> I may give the impression that the human being is completely and unavoidably influenced by his surrounding.

(In this case the surroundings being the unique structure of camp life, which forced the prisoner to conform his conduct to a certain set pattern.) But what about human liberty? Is there no spiritual freedom in regard to behavior and reaction to any given surroundings? . . . Does man have no choice of action in the face of such circumstances?

. . . The experiences of camp life show that man does have a choice of action. There were enough examples, often of a heroic nature, which proved that apathy could be overcome, irritability suppressed. Man *can* preserve a vestige of spiritual freedom, of independence of mind, even in such terrible conditions of psychic and physical stress.

We who lived in concentration camps can remember the men who walked through the huts comforting others, giving away their last piece of bread. They may have been few in number, but they offer sufficient proof that everything can be taken from a man but one thing: the last of the human freedoms—to choose one's attitude in a given set of circumstances, to choose one's own way. (Viktor E. Frankl, *Man's Search for Meaning* [Boston: Beacon Press, 1992], 74–75; emphasis in original)

Frankl and others in similar circumstances observed that moral agency could be maintained in even the most deplorable conditions if the human spirit willed it.

Second-Order Moral Agency

Let's consider the notion of second-order moral agency. Second-order moral agency involves the behavior of individuals toward the government and the social institutions under which they live. Latter-day Saints are familiar with the twelfth article of faith, which states that "we believe in being subject to kings, presidents, rulers, and magistrates, in obeying, honoring, and sustaining the law." The tenet is clear. Not only must we exercise our moral agency and obey the Ten Commandments, but we must also obey the political laws of the land. We cannot argue, for example, that federal income taxes are somehow immoral and illegal and cite religious agency as our defense.

Nevertheless, under many political systems second-order moral agency does present some inevitable moral dilemmas. For example, Americans appropriately revere their founding fathers for overthrowing a repressive government to replace it with one that would more fully guarantee certain freedoms. Their actions would clearly not fit into the category of sustaining the king. Consider also the circumstances faced by faithful Latter-day Saints living in Germany during World War II. They were required to fight in Hitler's army even though most of them were convinced the war was terribly immoral. Many did indeed fight. Some chose to flee.

Similarly, Brigham Young faced a dilemma when he was asked by the federal government to provide troops for what would be known as the Mormon Battalion march to California. The Saints had been driven from their homes, and ultimately they were forced to flee the United States to seek religious freedom outside the country. (In 1847, Mexico owned the area we now know as Utah.) Despite lack of support and protection from the federal government, President Young acceded to the request and called for volunteers. His inspiration to support the government when he could have rightfully refused proved to be a blessing to the Saints.

The concept of agency and how Latter-day Saints ought to relate to governments was clearly an issue for the Prophet Joseph Smith and the early Saints. The head note to Doctrine and Covenants 134 describes the section as "a declaration of belief regarding governments and laws in general, adopted by unanimous vote at a general assembly of the Church held at Kirtland, Ohio,

August 17, 1835." To the section was attached a preamble that stated, "That our belief with regard to earthly governments and laws in general may not be misinterpreted nor misunderstood, we have thought proper to present at the close of this volume our opinion concerning the same."

The Prophet Joseph felt it necessary to state to members and nonmembers alike that the Church intended to "sustain and uphold the respective governments in which they reside, while protected in their inherent and inalienable rights by the laws of such governments" (D&C 134:5).

In our current day, the Church has attempted to scrupulously adhere to the laws of the more than 170 countries of the world in which the Church currently operates. The practice of the Church when establishing a presence in a country is to go through the front door, not the back door. In other words, the Church seeks official recognition before beginning any operations; it does not attempt to surreptitiously fly under the radar of any sovereign entity. This policy has blessed the Church and its members on countless occasions.

The exercise of moral agency is not always easy—whether we're using first-order moral agency with respect to individuals or second-order moral agency with respect to governments. Undoubtedly we were taught in our premortal existence that it would not be a simple matter to make correct choices in every set of circumstances. Moral dilemmas will continue to exist for conscientious Latter-day Saints. Nevertheless, I believe we were enthusiastic to receive the opportunity to choose and become more like God in the process.

I have argued that God's plan for His children—that they learn to choose between good and evil—operates independently of the political system in which the people are required to live.

The fact that God gave men moral agency does not mean that

it can be exercised *only* in a government that recognizes personal liberty or free agency. Further, the gift of moral agency cannot be interpreted to be free agency and then used to argue that democracy, which promotes liberty, is the highest and best form of government. (In one sense that argument can appropriately be made, but on a different basis, as we discuss below.) Some obvious difficulties exist with the democratic form of government. Democracy as a political system, where decisions are made by the will of the people, has at least one major shortcoming. Let me illustrate.

Suppose two islands lie side by side in a large expanse of ocean. Both have direct democracies in which all citizens participate fully and cast informed votes on every important issue. The two islands communicate with one another, but they do not trade goods or services with each other.

One year a set of unusual conditions brings a near total crop failure to one island, which threatens to starve many of its people. The only source of available aid is from the neighboring island. But in order to provide that aid, the neighboring island must substantially raise its taxes. When the island follows its fully democratic process and brings the income tax measure to a vote, the measure is voted down because no one wants an increase in taxes. Their decision results in the death of many people.

In this admittedly simplistic example, one could find valid arguments why in the long run it would be in the best interest of the island not affected by the problem to do the right thing and vote to help its neighbors. But that is exactly the point of the story. Democracies are not somehow required by law to do the morally correct thing. The democratic process is a process of government designed to establish laws according to the will of the people, *be they moral or immoral.*

A marvelously lucid exposition of this simple truth is found in the Book of Mormon. Mosiah, who was the king, proposed that the people be ruled no more by kings but by judges who would be chosen by the voice of the people. He observed that "because all men are not just it is not expedient that ye should have a king or kings to rule over you. For behold, how much iniquity doth one wicked king cause to be committed, yea, and what great destruction!" (Mosiah 29:16–17).

After providing a perfect description of how iniquitous rulers maintain power (see verses 21 through 23), Mosiah said:

> And now behold I say unto you, it is not expedient that such abominations should come upon you.
>
> Therefore, *choose you by the voice of this people,* judges, that ye may be judged according to the laws which have been given you by our fathers, which are correct, and which were given them by the hand of the Lord.
>
> *Now it is not common that the voice of the people desireth anything contrary to that which is right; but it is common for the lesser part of the people to desire that which is not right; therefore this shall ye observe and make it your law—to do your business by the voice of the people.*
>
> And if the time comes that the voice of the people doth choose iniquity, then is the time that the judgments of God will come upon you; yea, then is the time he will visit you with great destruction. (Mosiah 29:24–27; emphasis added)

Mosiah makes the point very clearly. When government is by the voice of the people, the prerequisite for success is that they have a very well-defined notion of right and wrong. Democracies lead to no better results than dictatorships if the people do not exercise moral agency and make correct choices between good and evil.

Democracy may well be the best form of government that man, with the help of God, can devise. The United States form of democracy (more precisely, a representative republic) is based on a constitution that was established "by the hands of wise men whom I [God] raised up unto this very purpose" (D&C 101:80). Whether we speak of an inspired constitution or inspired men who wrote a constitution, it is clear that God had a hand in the form of government that would provide a setting most conducive to the restoration of the gospel.

Nevertheless, we also know that the final, highest, and best form of government will not be a democracy but a theocracy: a political structure where God rules over men. In such a government individual agency will be honored as it has been from the beginning. But the majority of the people will not be allowed to pervert that agency, as might be the case in a democracy.

Democracy, then, is the *second* best form of government that God both encourages and suffers to exist. Indeed, democracy could be thought of as a preparatory political system in the same way that the Aaronic Priesthood is preparatory to the Melchizedek Priesthood.

If democracy is an imperfect and preparatory form of government, should Latter-day Saints wait patiently and inertly for the ultimate theocracy, which has Christ at its head? Patiently, yes, but inertly—definitely not! The Church offers some insightful counsel to its members about exercising agency in political matters. The counsel begins by stating that the Church as an institution is politically neutral: "The Church's mission is to preach the Gospel of Jesus Christ, not to elect politicians. The Church of Jesus Christ of Latter-day Saints is neutral in matters of party politics. This applies to all of the many nations in which it is established" (see Political Neutrality, Public Issues, at www.newsroom.lds.org). The

political neutrality of the institutional church is further underscored by enumerating things the Church *does not do.*

> The Church does not:
> —Endorse, promote, or oppose political parties, can-
> didates, or platforms.
> —Allow its church buildings, membership lists, or
> other resources to be used for partisan political
> purposes.
> —Attempt to direct its members as to which candi-
> dates or party they should vote for. This policy
> applies whether or not a candidate for office is a
> member of The Church of Jesus Christ of Latter-
> day Saints.
> —Attempt to direct or dictate to a government leader.
> (see Political Neutrality, Public Issues, at www
> .newsroom.lds.org)

In addition, members are counseled about their individual
responsibility to exercise political agency.

> The Church does:
> —Encourage its members to play a role as responsible
> citizens in their communities, including becoming
> informed about issues and voting in elections.
> —Expect its members to engage in the political
> process in an informed and civil manner, respecting
> the fact that members of the Church come from a
> variety of backgrounds and experiences and may
> have differences of opinion in partisan political
> matters.
> —Request that candidates for office not imply that

their candidacy or platforms are endorsed by the
Church.

Quite clearly, members of the Church are encouraged to exercise political agency by being active in the political process. In the
United States, and increasingly in other countries of the world,
Latter-day Saints in political positions are found at all levels of
government. The relationship these political leaders have with the
Church is spelled out as follows: "Elected officials who are Latter-
day Saints make their own decisions and may not necessarily be in
agreement with one another or even with a publicly stated Church
position. While the Church may communicate its views to them,
as it may to any other elected official, it recognizes that the officials
still must make their own choices based on their best judgment
and with consideration of the constituencies whom they were
elected to represent" (see Political Neutrality, Public Issues, at
www.newsroom.lds.org).

One final point ought to be made. Earlier we discussed the
truth that God expects His children to choose right from wrong,
or exercise first-order moral agency, regardless of the political
system in which they find themselves. But the obligation of Latter-
day Saints goes beyond choosing and extends to being the leaven
in the loaf and light on the hill spoken of in the scriptures.
President Gordon B. Hinckley said:

> This entire people have become as a city upon a hill
> which cannot be hid. . . .
> Unless the world alters the course of its present trends
> (and that is not likely); and if, on the other hand, we
> continue to follow the teachings of the prophets, we shall
> increasingly become a peculiar and distinctive people of
> whom the world will take note. For instance, as the

integrity of the family crumbles under worldly pressures, our position on the sanctity of the family will become more obvious and even more peculiar in contrast, if we have the faith to maintain that position. . . .

It is not always easy to live in the world and not be a part of it. We cannot live entirely with our own or unto ourselves, nor would we wish to. We must mingle with others. In so doing, we can be gracious. We can be inoffensive. We can avoid any spirit or attitude of self-righteousness. But we can maintain our standards. The natural tendency will be otherwise, and many have succumbed to it. . . .

We can maintain the integrity of our families if we will follow the counsel of our leaders. As we do so, those about us will observe with respect and be led to inquire how it is done.

We can oppose the tide of pornography and lasciviousness, which is destroying the very fiber of nations. We can avoid partaking of alcoholic beverages and drugs and stand solidly for measures designed to lessen their use. As we do so, we shall find others who feel as we do and who will join hands in the battle.

We can more fully care for our own who may be in need rather than pass the burden to government and thereby preserve the independence and dignity of those who must have and are entitled to help.

We can refrain from buying on the Sabbath day. With six other days in the week, none of us needs to buy furniture on Sunday. None of us needs to buy clothing on Sunday. With a little careful planning we can easily avoid the purchase of groceries on Sunday.

As we observe these and other standards taught by the

Church, many in the world will respect us and find strength to follow that which they too know is right. . . .

We need not compromise. We must not compromise. The candle that the Lord has lighted in this dispensation can become as a light unto the whole world, and others seeing our good works can be led to glorify our Father in Heaven and emulate in their own lives the examples they have observed in ours.

Beginning with you and me, there can be an entire people who, by the virtue of our lives in our homes, in our vocations, even in our amusements, can become as a city upon a hill to which men may look and learn, and an ensign to the nations from which the people of the earth may gather strength. ("A City upon a Hill," *Ensign*, July 1990, 4–5)

The Church as an institution recognizes it also has a responsibility to not simply be neutral when it comes to moral issues. Quoting from the previously cited newsroom document, "The Church does: Reserve the right as an institution to address, in a nonpartisan way, issues that it believes have significant community or moral consequences or that directly affect the interests of the Church."

It is important to restate two key ideas we have developed here. The first is that the commandment to exercise moral agency is independent of the political system in which an individual finds himself. God's desire that His children come to know good from evil and act on that knowledge has been the same for all His children throughout the ages. The Ten Commandments were given as a standard for moral behavior and were meant to be followed regardless of the political system of government found in any given period. Does God favor democracy over other manmade forms of government? He well may do so. But knowing good from evil and acting morally is not inherent in any particular political form of government. A benevolent despot may actually provide an environment for exceptional moral behavior.

The second idea is companion to the first. God's gift of agency was and is the gift of moral agency. *The gift was not unbridled "free agency."* A democracy may be the form of government that engenders the greatest amount of individual freedom. But that freedom may also allow the greatest latitude for immoral behavior, should the people act according to their own wills. Thus, God's gift of moral agency does not necessarily install democracy as the most desirable political form of government. Stated another way, democracy is not inherently morally superior to any other form of government. Democracy is only as good or as bad as its people.

Having said that, Latter-day Saints have a responsibility to exercise their agency and both to practice and to promote morally correct principles in the communities and nations in which they live.

CHAPTER SEVEN

Economic Agency

Nothing is more to be prized, nor more sacred, than man's free choice. Free choice is the essence of free enterprise. It recognizes that the common man will make choices in his own self-interest. It allows a manufacturer to produce what he wants, how much, and to set his own price. It allows the buyer to decide if he wants a certain product at the price established. It preserves the right to work when and where we choose. (*Teachings of Ezra Taft Benson* [Salt Lake City: Bookcraft, 1988], 627)

THESE WORDS OF President Benson, who prior to becoming the President of the Church served as Secretary of Agriculture in the Eisenhower administration, describe the feelings of many Latter-day Saints toward economic agency. When I recently visited with colleagues at Brigham Young University, our discussion turned to the strong entrepreneurial orientation we observed in our students, as well as in Latter-day Saints in general. One colleague paused for a moment and then said, as nearly as I can recall, "It's in our genes, our spiritual DNA. We are risk takers from the beginning. We chose to take the risks associated with coming to earth. The other plan was the certain plan. *We were spiritual risk takers then and are earthy entrepreneurial risk takers now.*"

After some reflection, another colleague observed that all who have come to earth took the same risk; therefore, if there is something unusual about Latter-day Saints, it must be the teachings of the Church about agency, self-sufficiency, and individual responsibility. The discussion concluded with a general agreement that President Benson's statement about free enterprise reflects the views of many Latter-day Saints, who see a strong link between "free" agency and free enterprise. Most people would agree that if democracy is the political embodiment of agency, then free enterprise must be the economic embodiment.

Free enterprise, or economic free agency, as a means to order the production of goods and services in a society is a relatively new idea in the annals of history. For most of recorded time individuals lived in an agrarian setting with family members producing their own food, clothing, and shelter. Certain tasks were undertaken according to gender or tradition, and little agency was involved. Large community projects were directed by an authoritarian leader, and specific skills or trades were passed from father to son. In general, the supply of bricklayers, silversmiths, potters, tailors, and so forth was governed by the number of sons born to the men in those trades. (For an excellent exposition of these ideas, see Robert L. Heilbroner, *The Making of Economic Society* [Englewood Cliffs, New Jersey: Prentice Hall, 1985].)

It was not until the 1600s that the notion of economic agency began to appear. Later, in 1776, the Scottish economist Adam

Smith wrote in his book *The Wealth of Nations* about the novel concept that the macroeconomic interests of society could best be served by having each individual choose what was best for his or her micro interests. The result of individual self-determined decisions about production and consumption was the so-called "invisible hand" that produced the best results for the larger society.

The modern embodiment of free enterprise as a system for ordering the economic activities of a society (called capitalism) has been an overwhelming success at producing goods and services. One reason that capitalism is so successful at producing goods and services is that it unleashes the individual creativity and productive capacity of the people in the system. When individual agency and energy are not constrained and economic rewards are free to flow to individuals in proportion to their efforts, there are enormous potential material benefits to society. Admittedly, at an individual level we observe educational, political, geographical, and other constraints that restrict participation in the full benefits of a system of economic agency. In general, the more a society can eliminate constraints and allow full participation by each of its citizens, the better off all will be.

One of the results of an agency-based free-enterprise system is that material goods are distributed roughly according to ability and effort. The distribution is approximately normal or has the familiar bell shape shown in figure 7–1.

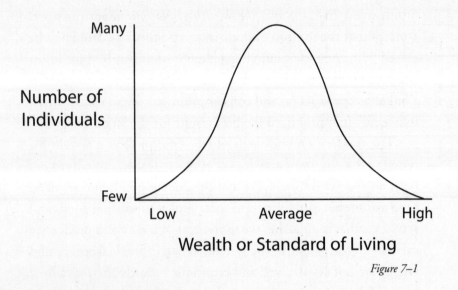

Figure 7–1

In figure 7–1, the standard of living is measured along the horizontal axis and ranges from poor (or a low standard of living) on the left to rich (or high standard of living) on the right. In this normal distribution, a few individuals are very poor and a few are very rich, while the majority have an average wealth and standard of living.

One problem with this kind of ability-based distribution is that of perceived equity or fairness. It doesn't seem "fair" that some are very rich and some are very poor. The problem is exacerbated by the observation that though the system favors agency, many of the rich and poor are that way through no merit or fault of their own. A major objective of a planned or socialistic economy is to address the material inequality resulting from capitalism.

Generally, we observe that in socialist or communist societies the goal is to have no rich or poor and to force everyone through various means to the same level of wealth or the same standard of living. The result is a tight or narrow distribution as shown in figure 7–2.

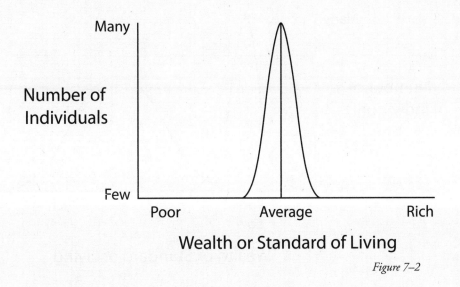

Figure 7–2

Figure 7–2 depicts a society in which very few are poor or rich and nearly everyone is average. At first glance this would seem to be a desirable outcome. But, in reality, policies that produce a narrow distribution of wealth also restrict the energy, motivation, and agency of individuals. The result is that while everyone is close to the average, the average is moved so far to the left that the overall standard of living is typically very low. Cuba and North Korea are currently the best examples of this kind of outcome. This problem ultimately proved the undoing of the former Soviet Union.

To further illustrate, the two figures are combined in the same graph in figure 7–3. In figure 7–3, the result of unconstrained economic agency is shown on the right as the same bell-shaped curve depicted in figure 7–1. On the left is the narrow distribution just discussed in figure 7–2.

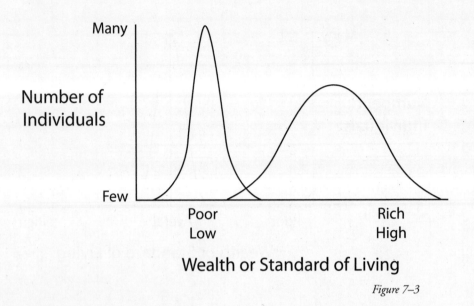

Figure 7–3

The curves have been deliberately drawn so that the poorest in the high standard-of-living society have about the same standard of living as nearly all of the population in the low standard-of-living society. As drawn, roughly 95 percent of the population in the wealthy society is better off than any or all of the population in the poorer society. In practice, the exact shapes of the curves and the relative positions of the averages along the continuum can be debated, but the general outcome is as shown.

What about the Poor?

In a society characterized by unconstrained economic agency, how acceptable is a wide divergence between the very rich and the very poor? In such an arrangement where wealth roughly mirrors ability and effort, does anyone have any responsibility for the poor? One approach is for society to recognize that some are disadvantaged as to their ability to contribute to the productivity of the society and share in its rewards. This disadvantage can flow from a variety of causes, including training, education, health, prejudice, and so forth. Programs are then instituted to address these problems. The programs are paid for through taxes that redistribute some the wealth from the more wealthy to the least wealthy. The hope is that, even though the government is taking some of the wealth from the rich, the rich will retain enough incentive and economic agency to keep the average standard of living from drifting downward. The number and extent of government-instituted programs are a reasonable measure of more or less "socialism" in a society. Government programs are mandated, and participation is usually required by law. To choose not to participate is not an option.

There is another, very different solution to the problem of the wide divergence of ability and subsequent wealth found in an unconstrained economic agency. That approach is charity. Those with more ability and resources can voluntarily exercise their agency and give to those who have less. For this approach to be effective, those who need help must somehow come to the attention of those willing to provide that help. In modern, complex societies the matching of the needy with charitable resources is problematic at best. Even the most charitable societies, of which the United States is one, also recognize the importance of mandated social programs at some basic level.

Notwithstanding the issue of how resources are distributed, the historical record is quite conclusive. From the perspective of the production of goods and services, modern capitalism is unquestionably the most successful economic system ever employed. The failure of capitalism's most recent competitor, namely communism, is well documented. The stark contrast between the economic might of South Korea and the abject poverty of North Korea, and the similar contrast between West and East Germany, drives home the impact of different economic

systems on identical populations. Zimbabwe and Venezuela will
soon be additional textbook examples of how destroying economic
agency and incentive can bankrupt a country and impoverish its
people.

We are currently in the midst of a fascinating economic experiment that is playing out on the world stage. I speak of China.
China is interesting for many reasons, but it is especially so in the
context of agency. In the past century, communism has been practiced in a number of countries. To my knowledge, it has always
been both a political system and an economic system. In other
words, those living under communism have neither had a voice in
the choosing of political leaders and policies, nor have they had a
say in production, marketing, or pricing decisions. Political and
economic communisms have gone hand in hand.

Modern China is attempting to sever that linkage. China's
leaders have launched the country into uncharted territory.
Communist party leaders are maintaining strict political control
and at the same time are allowing a form of free-market capitalism
to operate in the production of goods and services. The result is an
unbelievable surge in productivity and the standard of living
throughout the nation. The impact of the Chinese experiment is
being felt around the world as production is outsourced to Chinese
workers and raw material prices are dramatically impacted.

Importance of Morality to Free Enterprise

But just as democracy as a political system cannot deliver on
its promise without the exercise of moral agency, so it is with the
free-enterprise system. Whether in Utah, Russia, South America,
North Korea, or China, when a people embrace economic agency
without also embracing moral agency, things go badly. Having a
people capable of making morally correct choices is as important
to a free-market economic system as it is to a democratic political

system. Ample evidence exists that a society that will not establish and exercise principles of honesty and integrity eventually descends into corruption, bribery, and moral decay when it attempts to implement economic agency.

Adam Smith, one of the first to recognize economic agency and the "invisible hand," was also one of the first to recognize the importance of moral agency. Before writing his more famous book, *The Wealth of Nations,* in 1759 he wrote *The Theory of Moral Sentiments.* The two books together suggest that moral agency is a prerequisite to successful capitalism.

John Maynard Keynes, the noted twentieth-century English economist, observed when dealing with the economic malaise of his day, "What we need therefore in my opinion is not a change in our economic programmes. . . . No, what we need is the restoration of right moral thinking—a return to proper moral values in our social philosophy" (John Maynard Keynes, *The Collected Writings, vol. XXVII: Activities, 1940–1946,* ed. Donald Moggridge [New York: Cambridge University Press, 1980], 355). The right moral thinking that Keynes called for is not endemic to a system of free enterprise. It must be supplied from without by the individual moral behavior of those who wish to have the maximum benefits offered by a free-enterprise system.

In chapter six we noted that God intends His children to exercise moral agency regardless of the political system in which they find themselves. In just the same manner that the exercise of moral agency is independent of any political system, individuals can learn to distinguish good from evil and exercise moral agency in more than one particular economic order. The first-order moral imperatives concerning lying, stealing, covetousness, and honoring the Sabbath day are binding on individuals in a communist economy, socialist economy, capitalist economy, or any other kind of economy.

"Are you honest in your dealings with your fellowman?" is a question that God has expected to be answered in the affirmative from the time of Adam in Eden to Boris in Moscow.

There is another important point to be made relative to agency and capitalism. We cannot confuse moral agency with free agency and then use free agency as the doctrinal justification for a particular economic system. This is an especially important point to be understood by those who espouse free-market capitalism. Capitalism is hands down the most successful system the world has seen for freeing the creativity and capacity of individuals to produce goods and services. But capitalism it not perfect. It has warts.

In an unpublished paper titled *Church Leaders on Property, Wealth and the Economic Order*, Professor Phil Bryson of the BYU Marriott School of Business compares some of the writings of Hugh Nibley with those of the prophets of this dispensation. Professor Nibley was an outspoken critic of the abuses of capitalism. In one particularly colorful passage he exclaimed:

> When I find myself called upon to stand up and be counted, to declare myself on one side or the other, which do I prefer—gin or rum, cigarettes or cigars, tea or coffee, heroin or LSD, the Red Rose or the White, Shiz or Coriantumr, wicked Nephites or wicked Lamanites, Whigs or Tories, . . . land pirates or sea pirates, commissars or corporations, *capitalism or communism?* The devilish neatness and simplicity of the thing is the easy illusion that I am choosing between good and evil, when in reality two or more evils by their rivalry distract my attention from the real issue. (*Approaching Zion* [Salt Lake City: FARMS and Deseret Book, 1989], 163; emphasis added)

The real issue for Professor Nibley was that greed, the love of money, private property, and the accumulation of obscene wealth were abuses promoted by capitalism. Professor Bryson countered by pointing out in his paper that despite its shortcomings, the free-enterprise system has been uniformly supported by the leaders of the Church in this dispensation. He then made the observation, "In rejecting capitalism, the scholar [referring to Professor Nibley] overlooks the possibility that it is a lower order gift of God."

This is indeed the case. It is appropriate to point out that a free-market capitalistic economy is the economic expression of free agency (but not *moral agency*, as has already been argued) and could easily be deemed a *lower order gift of God*. But capitalism as we know it today, despite its successes, will not be the economic system under which we will ultimately live. The Lord has made clear that under His direction we will have an economic system superior to capitalism for blessing lives. It will be enjoyed by all those who have grown in spiritual maturity and the love of their fellowmen.

The scriptures provide two examples of such a system. The first was in the days of Enoch and the city of Zion. "And the Lord called his people ZION, because they were of one heart and one mind, and dwelt in righteousness; and there was no poor among them" (Moses 7:18). The second example is the nearly two hundred years of utopia experienced following the visit of the Savior to the Nephites on the American continent. Conditions in that period were described in Fourth Nephi: "And there were no contentions and disputations among them, and every man did deal justly one with another. And they had all things common among them; therefore there were not rich and poor, bond and free, but they were all made free, and partakers of the heavenly gift" (4 Nephi 1:2–3).

In the Millennium, agency will flourish. But it will be the

unbridled exercise of moral agency, not free agency, that will bring to pass the utopian conditions that are so anticipated. Under consecration, self-interest, the great incentive of markets and capitalism, will be replaced by the superior motivations of service and love.

Meanwhile, Latter-day Saints who understand the importance of exercising moral agency have several responsibilities, regardless of the economic system in which they live. The first of these is to be an example of morally correct behavior. God expects His children, who are to use this mortal probation to learn to become like Him, to learn the difference between right and wrong in all things economic. It is sad enough when someone extends the notion of agency to that of license and presumes that any behavior that is not specifically illegal is thereby justified. It is sadder still when that kind of behavior is exhibited by Latter-day Saints. We ought to know better and do better. We have a responsibility to distinguish clearly between what is morally acceptable and what is unacceptable, even if it has not yet been codified as illegal. We must understand that God's agency is moral agency and make economic decisions accordingly.

President Gordon B. Hinckley observed:

> Integrity is the very heart of commerce in the world in which we live. . . . Without personal integrity, there can be no confidence. Without confidence there can be no prospect of permanent success.
>
> No nation can either become or remain great if there is an absence of integrity in its citizens. . . . How much greater would be our appreciation of business if we knew that integrity was the basis for all commercial activity. (*Teachings of Gordon B. Hinckley* [Salt Lake City: Deseret Book, 1997], 267)

President Hinckley makes it clear that integrity and honesty in personal business dealings is essential to permanent success in economic affairs. Integrity in business is expected of every Latter-day Saint.

The second responsibility is to be generous with our means. In a free-enterprise system, we may be blessed because of ability and hard work or simply because of good fortune. In either case, we will be further blessed if we exercise agency to give of our time, talents, and resources to those who need our help. The Savior instructed His disciples, "Freely ye have received, freely give" (Matthew 10:8). That injunction would be important to heed in any economic system, but it is even more so in a free-enterprise system that provides such abundance to so many.

President Benson was right: "Nothing is more to be prized, nor more sacred than man's free choice." Free enterprise or a market-based economy may well be the economic embodiment of agency. Free-enterprise economies can provide great material benefits to most of their citizens. However, the poor cannot be neglected, and the moral principles of honesty and integrity must provide the foundation upon which market economies are based. But with all its benefits, capitalism is still a lower order gift of God. It will be replaced in the Millennium by an economic order in which love and service replace self-interest. How great will be our blessings when it can be said of us, "And the Lord called his people ZION, because they were of one heart and one mind, and dwelt in righteousness; and there was no poor among them" (Moses 7:18).

CHAPTER EIGHT

Religious Agency

> We claim the privilege of worshiping Almighty God according to the dictates of our own conscience, and allow all men the same privilege, let them worship how, where, or what they may. (Articles of Faith 1:11)

THIS ARTICLE OF FAITH is a clear statement by the Prophet Joseph Smith that agency is to be honored in religious matters as much as in any others. Unfortunately, religious persecution is often more pronounced in history than political or economic persecution.

The history of religious agency, or rather the lack of such agency, is the history of many of the world's greatest conflicts. Religious intolerance has been the centerpiece of thousands of years of history between the Arabs and Jews. The driving force behind the crusades of the Middle Ages was the religious conflict between Christians and Arabs. Protestant and Catholic differences were at the foundation of the Inquisition, the Huguenot wars, and more recently the ongoing Catholic-Protestant war in Northern Ireland. The Israeli-Arab conflict of the last sixty years is a continuation of an age-old animosity that has religion at its roots.

Today the prominent opinion in modern Europe, held by a large proportion of the populace of every nation there, is that religion is the source of all of society's miseries. They articulate in great detail the current and ongoing conflicts between Catholics and Protestants, Christians and Jews, Christians and Arabs, Shiites and Sunnis, Arabs and Jews, and so forth. They suggest that throughout history more wars have been fought, more people have been killed, and more families have been destroyed for religious reasons than all others put together. They consider all organized religions to be evil, regardless of individual doctrines, and they seek for a secular society without any religious influence to stir up contention.

The war in heaven, as noted in chapter two, was fought over whether the children of God would have complete agency and the right to make their own choices. God's grant of agency to mankind was fully intended to extend to agency in religious beliefs, and He understood the consequences of that gift. It meant that He and His Son and the truth about their plan would be rejected by one-third of the hosts of heaven in the premortal world and countless millions of Father's children experiencing mortality. It could not be any other way; men could not be given agency in political or economic decisions but constrained as to religious beliefs. Such was not part of the plan.

The notion of religious agency was clearly understood by the Nephite society of Alma's day:

> But it came to pass in the latter end of the seventeenth
> year, there came a man into the land of Zarahemla, and

he was Anti-Christ, for he began to preach unto the people against the prophecies which had been spoken by the prophets concerning the coming of Christ.

Now there was no law against a man's belief; for it was strictly contrary to the commands of God that there should be a law which should bring men on to unequal grounds.

For thus saith the scripture: Choose ye this day, whom ye will serve. (Alma 30:6–8; emphasis added)

As stated in verse 7, *"There was no law against a man's belief; for it was strictly contrary to the commands of God that there should be a law which should bring men on to unequal grounds."*

Alma could not have been happy that Korihor was preaching against Christ and the prophets. Nevertheless, he explained that in his contemporary society, "There was no law against a man's belief." Without further clarification, we might suppose that this declaration of religious agency was an expression of an enlightened society. But this was not the case. Instead, Alma stated explicitly that it was "strictly contrary to the commands of God" that men should be treated unequally because of their beliefs. In other words, the injunction against punishing a man for his beliefs came from God.

After explaining that there was no Nephite law against a man's belief, Alma reaffirmed in verse 8 the extraordinary tenet and attitude of a loving Heavenly Father. "For thus saith the scripture: Choose ye this day, whom ye will serve." Alma recognized that God intended man to have religious agency—he would be free to choose whether or not to serve God or, for that matter, whether to believe in any God or no God. In addition, man would not be coerced toward any belief by threat of punishment.

This point is reiterated in the verse that follows: "Now if a man desired to serve God, it was his privilege; or rather, if he believed in God it was his privilege to serve him; *but if he did not believe in him there was no law to punish him*" (Alma 30:9; emphasis added). In other words, in Nephite society people would have true religious freedom.

It is important to note that despite the existence of religious freedom in Nephite society, the law provided a clear incentive for making correct moral choices. The moral law was interpreted consistent with the first-order moral agency framework of the Ten Commandments discussed earlier. We read in Alma: "But if he murdered he was punished unto death; and if he robbed he was also punished; and if he stole he was also punished; and if he committed adultery he was also punished; yea, for all this wickedness they were punished" (Alma 30:10).

So Nephite law recognized that some actions were morally unacceptable and would be punished. But religious beliefs did not fall into that category. Alma records: "For there was a law that men should be judged according to their crimes. Nevertheless, there was no law against a man's belief; therefore, a man was punished only for the crimes which he had done; therefore all men were on equal grounds" (Alma 30:11).

The law made it clear that religious beliefs of whatever kind were not a crime and could not be the basis for any punishment. Therefore, men were on equal ground when it came to religious matters, and there was true religious agency in Nephite society.

Unfortunately, such was not the case in the early nineteenth-century society of the Prophet Joseph Smith. He experienced the sad irony that those who so adamantly seek religious freedom for themselves are often the first to deny it to others. The early Pilgrims and many others who came to America were motivated by the prospect of religious freedom. But the Prophet Joseph was persecuted from the time of his first vision to the end of his life, often by those who had sought religious agency for themselves but would not extend it to a "Mormon prophet."

The Prophet Joseph was acutely aware of this foible of human nature. His concern for this issue is reflected in the eleventh article of faith, which reads, "We claim the privilege of worshiping Almighty God according to the dictates of our own conscience, and allow all men the same privilege, let them worship how, where, or what they may." This article of faith is a clear statement that agency is to be honored in religious matters as much as in any other.

As Latter-day Saints we are constantly reminded by our leaders that our zeal for the restored gospel must not turn to lack of tolerance for other's beliefs or practices. For example, President Gordon B. Hinckley said, "We must work harder to build mutual respect, an attitude of forbearance, with tolerance one for another regardless of the doctrines and philosophies which we may espouse" (*Teachings of Gordon B. Hinckley* [Salt Lake City: Deseret Book, 1997], 665). On another occasion he encouraged us to "never forget that we live in a world of great diversity. The people of the earth are all our Father's children and are of many and varied religious persuasions. We must cultivate tolerance and appreciation and respect one another" (Gordon B. Hinckley, "The Work Moves Forward," *Ensign,* May 1999, 5).

Latter-day Saint religious beliefs are sufficiently intriguing to those of other Christian faiths that we will always be the object of discussion, criticism, and even derision. Early members of the Church were persecuted, mobbed, murdered, and driven from state to state and finally out of the boundaries of the United States by those who did not understand freedom of religion. If anyone should understand the importance of tolerance in religious matters it should be Latter-day Saints. We must not return derision for derision or intolerance for intolerance. Religious intolerance is not part of the gospel of Christ, it is not in the doctrine of His restored Church, and it should not be in the practice of any of its members.

Parents and Religious Agency

It is interesting to observe how current Church members handle the issue of religious agency in relation to their children. In this, as in many issues, there seem to be two extremes. On one end of the spectrum is the notion that children ought to be allowed very early on to make their own decision about whether or not to attend church on Sunday or other Church-related activities. The notion is that if a child does not want to go to church for whatever reason, don't force him or her. If they don't like Primary or sacrament meeting, they shouldn't have to go. After all, agency must be honored; children should be able to choose their clothes, their hairstyle, and their Church activity.

At the other extreme is the very strict, "agency and how to enforce it" authoritarian approach. Children *will* go to church, they *will* stay in their Sunday clothes all day, they *will not* play outside, and their inside activities *will* be quiet scripture reading, journal writing, and other similar endeavors.

Neither of these extreme approaches is likely to achieve the desired outcome. Children need guidance and clear expectations, but they should not be coerced into resentment through heavy-handed techniques. Someone has said that successful parenting is taking children from the law of Moses to the Sermon on the Mount. The "thou shalts" and "thou shalt nots" of early childhood can be gradually replaced with behavior motivated by love and respect for both parents and the Lord.

Along the way from Moses to the Sermon on the Mount, parents can make good use of humor and psychology. One Sunday morning one of our teenage boys decided he was too tired to go to church and was going to stay in bed. Margaret was surprised because this was new behavior for this son. Her reaction became the stuff of family legend. She said, "I don't blame you. I'm tired too. Move over!" and she climbed into bed next to the recalcitrant son. After about two minutes he said, "Mom, this is totally lame" and he got up, got dressed, and went to church.

Children can be taught to love Church activities, love the Lord, and love to serve through the attitude of parents. Children will learn to exercise agency in religious matters by observing the behavior of their parents. A parent who criticizes a spouse for choosing to attend church, serve in a calling, go to the temple, or pay tithing will soon observe the children misunderstanding how God intends us to use the gift of agency.

Agency and Missionary Work

It is important for missionaries and all Church members to understand the role of agency in their missionary work. As I noted earlier, it is useful for them to understand that the operative word to be used in their work is *invite*. To "challenge" someone is inconsistent with the concept of agency and could be interpreted as being more combative than missionaries should wish to be perceived. An invitation to read, pray, and attend meetings honors agency. Where such invitations are accepted and acted upon, a foundation is laid from which a person can willingly embrace the commandments and prepare for baptism. When people recognize that they have, of their own free will, accepted an invitation—not a challenge—to be baptized, they are much more likely to choose to continue to be blessed by activity in the Church.

The same concept of invitation should be used when approaching inactive members. They should be invited to attend church; they should be invited to accept home and visiting teachers; they should be invited to remember the spiritual promptings that led them to their initial conversion. Such invitations respect their right to choose to return to activity and receive the blessings that accompany the exercise of agency.

For both potential converts and inactive members, continued encouragement is not inappropriate. Neither is promising the fulfillment of blessings that are found in the scriptures and reiterated by priesthood and sister leaders. Missionaries should pray for their investigators; parents should pray for their children and loved ones; members everywhere should pray for the truths of the gospel to be preached to all the world. Such prayers will not abrogate the agency of those for whom the prayers are offered.

Agency in the Millennium

Does the Church really believe in religious agency in the long run? When the opportunity presents itself, for example, in the Millennium, will religious agency still be honored? When our affairs are governed by a theocracy with Christ at the head, will all be forced to hold the same religious beliefs? The scriptures make it clear when He comes the second time He will come in His glory. Concerning that day, Paul told the Romans, "For it is written, As I live, saith the Lord, every knee shall bow to me, and every tongue shall confess" (Romans 14:11). In the day when every knee shall bow, will agency still be honored?

Some insight into the question is gained by reflecting on Doctrine and Covenants 20:17: "By these things we know that there is a God in heaven, who is infinite and eternal, from everlasting to everlasting the same unchangeable God, the framer of heaven and earth, and all things which are in them." God does not change. His gift of agency given in the premortal world and extended to Adam and his posterity in the garden will not be taken away when Christ comes in His glory.

Addressing this point Elder Bruce R. McConkie stated:

Since all who are living at least a terrestrial law—the law of honesty, uprightness, and integrity—will be able to abide the day of our Lord's coming, there will be nonmembers of the Church on earth during the millennium. Honest and upright people who have been deceived by the false religions and false philosophies of the world *will not have their free agency abridged.* They will continue to *believe their false doctrines* until they voluntarily elect to receive gospel light. (Bruce R. McConkie, *Mormon Doctrine,* 2nd ed. [Salt Lake City: Bookcraft, 1966], 498–99; emphasis added)

Elder McConkie clearly asserts that religious agency will not be abridged in the Millennium and that honest and upright people will be allowed to voluntarily elect to receive gospel light. Upon reflection, it would be illogical to suppose that God would change His mind about agency after having upheld the principle through an entire premortality marked by a heavenly war and through an entire mortality punctuated by the crucifixion of His Only Begotten Son. We should not doubt His commitment to the principle of agency, a gift given in love and intended to endure forever.

In addition, agency is often misused in mortality due to perverse incentives and incorrect and deceiving information. In the Millennium the source of deception will be constrained, and perverse incentives will be realigned to be in harmony with the principles of love and service.

The concept of religious agency is nicely summed up by a hymn by an anonymous author:

Know this, that ev'ry soul is free
To choose his life and what he'll be;

For this eternal truth is giv'n:
That God will force no man to heav'n.
He'll call, persuade, direct aright,
And bless with wisdom, love, and light,
In nameless ways be good and kind,
But never force the human mind.
        (*Hymns of The Church of Jesus Christ of*
        Latter-day Saints [1985], no. 240)

How grateful we should be for the incomparable gift of agency given to us by a loving Heavenly Father. It is a gift given to allow us to gain wisdom in religious matters as in all others; it is a gift that, if exercised correctly, will allow us when we see Him to be like Him.

CHAPTER NINE

Agency, Uncertainty, and Learning by Study

ONE DAY I made the mistake of describing to my oldest boys an incident from my childhood. I told them about being in the backyard with my father and noticing that he was looking intently at the willow tree on the edge of the patio. The tree seemed to be dying, if not already dead. With a twinkle in his eye, he asked me to go to the garage and bring back the tree saw. He took the saw and proceeded to cut off most of the branches until nothing was left but a trunk and two large branches that formed the shape of an eight-foot-tall letter Y. He then asked me to bring him an old bicycle inner tube, which he proceeded to cut into long strips of rubber. Next, he asked me for my old ball glove—and with a pair of scissors he cut the leather pocket away from the rest of the glove. He cut a slit in each side of the leather pocket, and then he fastened one end of a long strip of rubber to each side of the pocket. At that moment, I began to see where all this was leading. Dad got a ladder and tied each of the free ends of the giant rubber bands to the two top arms of the willow tree Y. Voila, he had made a giant slingshot.

He then invited me to go out to the garden and bring back several ripe tomatoes. "Oh, boy," I said to myself, "this is gonna be good." Dad put a tomato in the flipper pocket, pulled it back about eight feet, and let it fly. The tomato sailed out over the back hedge, over the house behind us, and was still gaining altitude when it went out of sight. At that point, Dad's shoulders shook with a huge chuckle, and I knew what he was thinking. He was thinking about an unsuspecting neighbor enjoying a quiet moment on the back patio when silently, out of nowhere, a tomato interrupted his reverie with an enormous splat!

I got quite a kick out of telling this story to the boys. Turns out, it became another in a long line of lessons on the principle of unintended consequences. Many years later, in an unguarded story-telling moment, one of the boys said, "Dad, do you remember that story you told us about your father and the giant backyard tomato flipper?" I acknowledged that I did.

The boys then proceeded to explain that not long after hearing the story, they decided to try their own hand at tomato flipping. They cut the pocket out of an old ball glove and attached to each side a six-foot length of surgical tubing. They correctly observed that in this particular application surgical tubing was far superior to rubber bicycle inner tubes. They decided that mobility would be a useful component of their plan. This would be achieved by putting two boys four feet apart with each holding one end of the tubing over his inside shoulder. The third boy would launch the tomato by pulling the pocket back between the two-boy "launching posts" and let it fly out between them toward the intended target.

They took their operation upstairs to our second-story master bedroom, which had a deck that was accessible through a large sliding glass door. One boy stood on one side of the deck with the tubing over his shoulder, one boy stood on the other side in a similar manner, and the third boy loaded the tomato and pulled it back through the door opening so it could sail out over the deck and beyond.

In their initial attempts, they were successful at sending the tomato over the backyard fence, but they really wanted to see if they could launch it clear over the backyard neighbor's house and into the street beyond. To do that, the launching boy realized that he would have to stretch the tubing farther. With a big, ripe tomato in the pouch, he achieved maximum firepower by pulling the tubing back through the sliding glass doors into the bedroom, back to the foot of the bed, and back still farther until he was lying on the bed with his head against the headboard. He let the pouch go and jumped off the bed to see the result. The pouch flew the width of the room, out the sliding glass doors, past the two boys holding the tubing.

Then, just as the tomato was about to be released from the pouch—the pouch turned around. The pouch, still containing the tomato, came back across the railing, back past the two boys, back through the sliding glass door—and, as the launching boy jumped off the bed, the tomato hit him full in the chest. The splat sent tomato everywhere—onto the wall, the ceiling, the curtains, the carpet, and the boy!

The boys said, "Dad, we spent two solid hours cleaning up the mess." They did such a good job we never knew what had happened.

In the same way that I had relearned the principle of unintended consequences, my sons had experienced the principle of unexpected outcomes.

Unintended consequences and unexpected outcomes are two

of the many expressions we use to describe the uncertainty that characterizes our mortal state. It is in the mortal laboratory of uncertainty that we learn through our own experience to develop the godlike traits of wisdom and judgment.

Consider the words engraved on the stairwell wall between the third and fourth floors of the Harold B. Lee Library at Brigham Young University. The words are:

> SEEK LEARNING,
> EVEN BY STUDY
> AND ALSO BY FAITH.
> D&C 88:118

A student may encounter that scripture many times during his or her stay at the university. Such a student may wish to forgo the difficulty of learning by study and simply try to figure out how to learn by faith. He or she may conclude that if the Lord wanted us to learn chemistry or calculus by faith, we should be able to furrow our brows, concentrate really hard on believing, and into our minds would come the formulas we need to know. Those who try to substitute faith for the study they should be doing usually find the results less than stellar. It turns out that learning by study and by our own experience is a major part of our Father's plan.

In this chapter we will examine the role that agency plays in learning by study—and the uncertainty that results from agency. In the next chapter we will investigate the interplay between agency and learning by faith.

As we learn by study, we must keep in mind that while we have been invited to "seek ye out of the best books words of wisdom" (D&C 88:118), we have also learned that the study of secular knowledge should not be our primary objective. The knowledge that God most desires us to obtain is the knowledge of good and evil. "For God doth know that in the day ye eat thereof, then your eyes shall be opened, and *ye shall be as gods, knowing good and evil.*" (Moses 4:11; emphasis added). *Knowing* good and evil, or developing *wisdom and judgment* concerning good and evil and their associated consequences, is the *learning* that God intends from our mortal experiences. Some have asked, how does agency help us become as God? The answer is that agency creates a set of conditions under which God's children are able to gain wisdom and judgment through study and experience.

To understand the relationship between agency and *uncertainty,* consider first the relationship between agency and *certainty.* A state of *certainty* can be defined as one in which an agent or intelligent being makes rational choices that are based upon a complete knowledge of all alternatives and all future outcomes associated with those alternatives. In such a world of certainty, there are no unexpected consequences, there is no opposition—and there is no development of the wisdom Eve desired (see Moses 4:12). Under conditions of certainty, agency does not result in the experience, wisdom, and judgment that God intended.

A state of *uncertainty* describes the one in which we operate in mortality. We continue as intelligent agents, but we have an incomplete knowledge of alternatives, as well as an incomplete knowledge of the outcomes and consequences associated with those alternatives.

As figure 9–1 reflects, agency exercised under conditions of uncertainty leads to learning right from wrong both by study and also by faith.

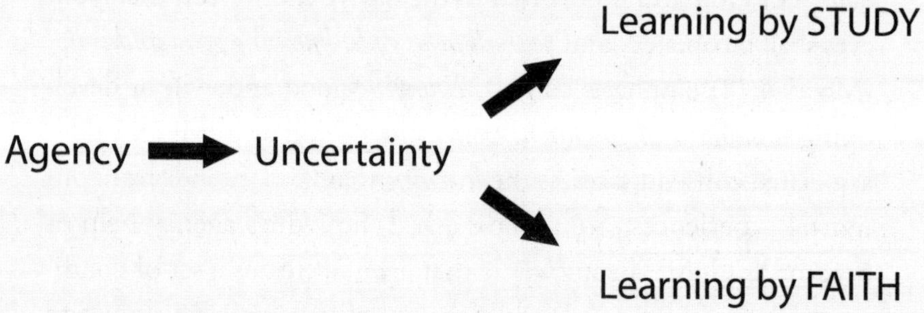

Learning by STUDY

Agency ➡ Uncertainty

Learning by FAITH

Figure 9–1

Exercising agency under uncertainty allows us to *learn by study and validate moral principles by our own experience.* It also allows us to learn by faith, which we will investigate in the next chapter.

Agency and Uncertainty

There is a strong link between the agency that God gave to man and the uncertainty that characterizes mortal experiences. Choosing under uncertainty is the cause of a great deal of learning in life, as well as a great deal of stress. Who has not at some time wished somebody else would step in and be responsible to make a particular hard choice? Or who has not wished to see into the future and thereby know what to do with all the agonizing analysis that characterizes decision making? And isn't uncertainty another name for risk? Isn't risk like gambling on the stock market or playing the horses—and something to be avoided and even shunned? No wonder we have consternation!

Yes, *risk* and *uncertainty* are close companions, and one should clearly not get involved in gambling! But keep in mind that the individual whose plan was to eliminate all uncertainty is not the good guy in the larger drama of life. His plan was rejected by God, which is one reason why it is useful to understand more about the plan that was chosen and under which we are operating.

The Savior's parable of the talents enhances our understanding of the plan that involves risk and uncertainty. The parable is introduced with the words, "For the kingdom of heaven is as . . ." (Matthew 25:14). Thus, the parable that follows promises to teach a principle whose application is not limited to this earth only.

After giving one, two, and five talents (a measure indicating money) to his servants to manage, the Lord (or owner) leaves on a journey. Upon his return he asks for an accounting of each servant's stewardship. The two-talent and five-talent servants are each able to report that they doubled their talents, and they each earn the praise of the Lord and the promise of great blessings to come. The one-talent servant returns the one talent with the explanation that he guarded it carefully out of fear. The narrative continues:

> His lord answered and said unto him, Thou wicked and slothful servant, thou knewest that I reap where I sowed not, and gather where I have not strawed:
>
> Thou oughtest therefore to have put my money to the exchangers, and then at my coming I should have received mine own with usury.
>
> Take therefore the talent from him, and give it unto him which hath ten talents.
>
> For unto every one that hath shall be given, and he shall have abundance: but from him that hath not shall be taken away even that which he hath.
>
> And cast ye the unprofitable servant into outer darkness: there shall be weeping and gnashing of teeth. (Matthew 25:26–30)

The one-talent servant clearly feared the uncertainty of putting his one talent to the money exchangers. His fear indicates that money given to the exchangers was at risk. But the response of the

Lord in the parable underscores that uncertainty is indeed part of the larger plan of life, a part that must be acknowledged.

Furthermore, his exhortation to cast the unprofitable servant into outer darkness is uncharacteristically harsh if we interpret it simply as a response to the loss of interest on a small investment. But Jesus is teaching that those who reject agency and uncertainty will be as the one-third who chose unwisely in the premortal existence. They will find themselves excluded from abundance in any kingdom of glory and cast into outer darkness.

The parable of the talents suggests that the notions of agency, choice, and uncertain outcomes are intertwined in ways that deserve further investigation. These ideas are best understood in a framework that requires less casual and more careful reading. Hopefully the insights will be proportional to the additional effort required.

Processes and Outcomes

Let's consider the notion of a process and the outcomes that result from that process. Some processes are designed to give a single, predictable outcome that is always the same. Gravity in its simple form is an example of such a process. Things always fall down, never up or sideways. Many other natural processes also have outcomes that are always the same and never vary. Processes with outcomes that are always the same are referred to as *deterministic* or *certain* processes, or we may speak of a process as having a deterministic or certain outcome. In either case, whether speaking of the process or the outcome, a deterministic process will always yield the same result; it never varies from one time to the next.

But many processes yield a different outcome each time the process is implemented. Picking a card from a deck of cards is such a process. Each time the process is implemented, the outcome or result of the process is different and unpredictable or uncertain. These processes are sometimes referred to as *random* processes, since the outcomes may appear to have no pattern and seemingly cannot be determined in advance.

One of the things we can learn about random processes, however, is that contrary to our first impression, the outcomes may have a central tendency. In other words, some outcomes show up more often than others, and some are very rarely, if ever, observed. We learn to say, "If I had to bet, I'd say that the likely outcome from that process is . . . ," or we may say, "Well, of course that could happen, but it's very unlikely or almost impossible so we won't worry about it."

We should observe in passing that we have recently developed very sophisticated statistical techniques to deal with random processes, but for most of the mortal time line these techniques were not available—and they are still not well-understood by most people. Instead, we seek to find individuals of "wisdom" and "judgment" to help us deal with uncertainty. We speak of the "wisdom of the ages" or we seek out a "wise old man" or "wise old woman" to shed light on the decision-making process.

These ideas can be illustrated visually through the use of figures and graphs. Such figures may resemble something from the reader's educational past that evokes an instant mental block. If that unpleasant reaction can be suppressed for a few minutes, the illustrations can be very helpful in understanding some fundamental concepts.

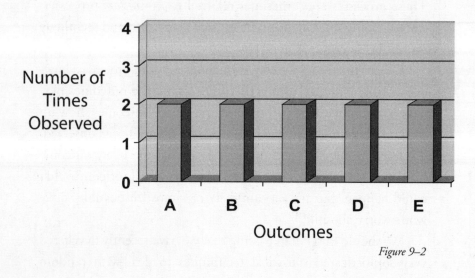

Figure 9–2

Figure 9–2 is a graph of something called process ONE, with outcomes A through E depicted on the horizontal axis. The frequency of the outcomes, or how often they occur, is depicted on the vertical axis. In the case of this particular process, outcome A occurs two times. Outcomes B through E also occur exactly two times each. In other words, when process one is observed ten times, the result is that each of the five possible outcomes is observed exactly two times. The outcomes are said to be "distributed" equally, meaning they each occur with the same frequency. The outcomes may also be said to be uniformly distributed or may be said to follow a uniform "distribution."

In a uniform distribution such as the one above, it is not possible to say that one outcome is more likely than another. Indeed, they are all equally likely. In one sense, uniform distributions are not very helpful. They leave us truly perplexed about what will be the outcome of the process. Fortunately, most processes have outcomes that are *not* uniformly distributed.

Figure 9–3 is a picture or graph of process TWO. Process TWO has five possible outcomes, just as does process ONE. However, the five outcomes in process TWO are distributed differently than those in process ONE.

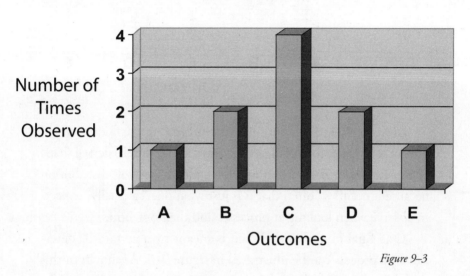

Process TWO

Figure 9–3

In process TWO, outcomes A and E each occur one time. Outcomes B and D each occur two times. But outcome C occurs four times. So the most likely outcome from process TWO is definitely outcome C. It is four times more likely to occur than either possibility A or E and twice as likely as either outcome B or D.

The shape formed by the tops of the bars in figure 9–3 may look somewhat familiar to the reader. That familiar shape is redrawn as a smooth curve in figure 9–4.

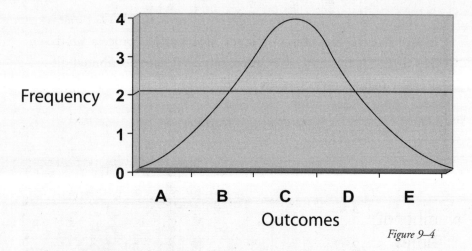

Figure 9–4

In figure 9–4, the various points representing the frequencies of each outcome are smoothed into a curve that has the classic bell shape of a so-called normal distribution. It is called a "normal" distribution because it occurs so often that it is just what one "normally" expects to observe when looking at processes and their outcomes.

One final observation: What is meant by a certain or deterministic process can be illustrated in figure 9–5. As shown in this figure, process THREE has outcome A as its only possible result.

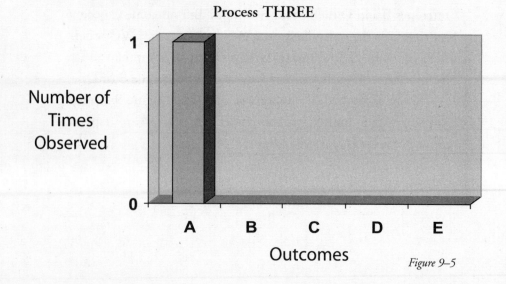

Figure 9–5

In other words, no matter how many times process THREE is observed, the outcome will always be A. It will never be anything else. Process THREE is like gravity. No matter how many times the apple is dropped it will always fall down, never up or sideways. Most of the physical phenomena observed on the earth (within the normal range of human observation) are deterministic processes. More will be said about this in chapter ten.

But most of the social (as opposed to physical) processes observed on the earth *do not have deterministic outcomes* but rather have the normally distributed outcomes shown in figures 9–3 and 9–4. The reason for that is agency.

President Spencer W. Kimball understood well that the program of the Father was intended to help His children gain wisdom and judgment. President Kimball recognized that deterministic outcomes are not the agency-based plan of the Father and that wisdom, judgment, character, joy, and happiness require uncertainty for their development. He said:

> Some become bitter when oft-repeated prayers seem unanswered. Some lose faith and turn sour when solemn administrations by holy men seem to be ignored and no restoration seems to come from repeated prayer circles. But if all the sick were healed, if all the righteous were protected and the wicked destroyed, the whole program of the Father would be annulled and *the basic principle of the gospel, free agency, would be ended.*
>
> If pain and sorrow and total punishment immediately followed the doing of evil, no soul would repeat a misdeed. If joy and peace and rewards were instantaneously given to the doer of good there could be no evil—all would do good and not because of the righteousness of doing good. There would be no test of strength, no development of

character, no growth of power, no free agency. There would also be an absence of joy, success, resurrection, eternal life, and godhood. (*Teachings of Spencer W. Kimball,* ed. Edward L. Kimball [Salt Lake City: Bookcraft, 1982], 77)

For further illustration of these ideas, let's consider the principle "Thou shalt not steal," and three possible scenarios that each illustrate an important idea. Each of the scenarios will use the idea of processes and outcomes to give more insight to the workings of agency and learning by study.

In the first scenario a thief chooses to steal. (Stealing, then, is the process we're looking at.) The outcome or consequence in this scenario is that he is caught immediately and both hands are cut off. This outcome happens every time without exception. Thus, in this scenario the process has only one outcome, and it is a perfectly certain outcome. This is the world of determinism. This is process THREE, shown earlier.

This is exactly the situation President Kimball described when he said, "If pain and sorrow and total punishment immediately followed the doing of evil, no soul would repeat a misdeed. If joy and peace and reward were instantaneously given to the doer of good there could be no evil—all would do good and not because of the righteousness of doing good. There would be no test of strength, no development of character, no growth of powers, and no free agency."

Now consider scenario two. In this scenario, when a thief steals there are only two possible outcomes: (A) no one ever finds out about it and the thief "gets away with it," or (B) the thief gets caught and is punished. Suppose in this scenario the outcomes are uniformly distributed. In other words, each outcome is equally likely, or each has a 50 percent chance of occurring.

Several observations can be made concerning this scenario. The first is that it is hard for a person in this setting to judge whether or not "thou shalt not steal" is a valid principle. If half the time you "get away with it" and half the time you don't, experience does not necessarily validate the "thou shalt not steal" principle. The second observation is that this is exactly how an inexperienced or untaught person may view the world. A person lacking experience and judgment may well suppose that stealing is just as likely to bring a reward as a punishment and therefore proceed to ignore the principle and steal.

The third scenario is much richer than the first two. In this scenario, when a thief steals there are five possible outcomes with different likelihoods. They are as follows:

(A) No one finds out and the thief gets away with it. This happens one out of every ten times.

(B) The thief gets caught but is allowed to apologize and make restitution. This happens two out of ten times.

(C) The thief is caught and is given the average punishment according to accepted sentencing guidelines. This happens four out of ten times.

(D) The thief is caught and receives the maximum and most severe punishment allowed by law. This occurs two out of ten times.

(E) The thief is caught in the act and is shot and killed. This happens one time in ten.

The first thing to notice in this third scenario is that multiple outcomes are possible. This is not the world of determinism that was proposed by Satan and rejected by the Father and Son and two-thirds of the hosts of heaven. It is rather the world of uncertainty that allows the development of wisdom and judgment envisioned in the Father's plan.

Notice also that the distribution across outcomes is not uniform but approximates the shape identified as "normal." The most likely outcome in scenario three, which occurs four out of ten times, is that the thief is caught and receives an average punishment. This happens four times more often than the outcome in which the thief gets away with it. This most likely outcome supports the underlying principle of "Thou shalt not steal." People with judgment and wisdom recognize that the principle is valid and is consistent with their experience. People with impaired judgment know someone who stole without getting caught and choose to steal based on the assumption that their own outcome will be like the single other outcome that they choose to focus on.

In this scenario most of the outcomes are bad. Seven of the ten possibilities are clearly bad outcomes. Outcome B is at best neutral. Thus the *accumulation* of the possibilities results in at least seven of ten outcomes being bad, and it could be argued that nine of the ten outcomes are something other than positive.

The introduction of the concept of *cumulative likelihoods* here is very important. Though the process in scenario three has five possible outcomes, for any one act of stealing only one of them actually happens and can be observed after the fact. So it is possible that an individual wishing to develop wisdom and judgment could observe the outcome from one particular stealing process and see only that the thief got away with it. Only after observing the outcomes from ten stealing processes could a well-informed judgment be made.

Thus, while knowing the most likely outcome is useful information, the rest of the available information is very helpful in understanding all possible outcomes and thus developing wisdom and judgment. *Wisdom and judgment are developed and tempered by accumulated experiences* that are either personal or observed. In scenario three, both the most likely outcome as well as the accumulated likelihoods support the morally correct principle, "Thou shalt not steal."

Note that the principle of time is important in the process. Not all outcomes are immediate. Being shot in the process of stealing is an immediate outcome, but the others take varying amounts of time to play out. Furthermore, the process has to be observed multiple times in order to see and understand all the possible outcomes and consequences. For most individuals, seeing or "experiencing" all the outcomes is a sequential process. In fact, that is exactly what is generally meant by experience. Someone with experience has had the benefit of seeing over time all the possible outcomes from a particular process. This person also has developed a sense of the likelihood of the occurrence of each outcome. Such a person is said to have good sense and judgment. He or she is considered to be wise and is sought after for counsel. It is not by chance that the wise person is also usually "old," for it takes the passage of time to accumulate all the observations on a given process.

If either time or outcomes were deterministic, we would not form our own judgment or develop wisdom concerning the principles in play. The fact that there is variance in the outcomes and also in the dimension of time is how we learn wisdom or learn to "decide with soundness, prudence and intelligence tempered by experience, training, and maturity" (our dictionary definition of wisdom).

The Role of Time

The fact that time is sequential is quite fascinating. It could be argued that if what we call past, present, and future were all before us at the same time, we would not need faith in Christ. We would see Him anointed as Savior, born as a babe, crucified, resurrected, coming in His glory, and sitting in judgment. All would be simultaneously before us. There would have been no need in either the premortal or mortal existence to have faith in the plan or in "the son of man."

While it is generally true that the passage of time goes hand in hand with the experience obtained through many observations, that it is not always the case. Elder David A. Bednar of the Quorum of the Twelve Apostles encouraged students at Brigham Young University–Idaho to be "Quick to Observe." He cited the example of the prophet Mormon:

> And now I, Mormon, make a record of the things which I have both seen and heard, and call it the Book of Mormon.
>
> And about the time that Ammaron hid up the records unto the Lord, he came unto me, (I being about ten years of age . . .) and Ammaron said unto me: I perceive that thou art a sober child, and art *quick to observe;*
>
> Therefore, when ye are about twenty and four years old I would that ye should remember the things that *ye have observed* concerning this people; . . .
>
> And behold, ye shall . . . engrave on the plates of Nephi all the things that *ye have observed* concerning this people.
>
> And I, Mormon, . . . remembered the things which Ammaron commanded me. (Mormon 1:1–5; emphasis added)

After quoting this passage, Elder Bednar said to the assembled students, "As you celebrate your graduation today and leave

BYU–Idaho, I hope you also have become 'quick to observe.' Your future success and happiness will, in large measure, be determined by the spiritual capacity to be quick to observe" ("Quick to Observe," BYU–Idaho 2004 Commencement, August 20, 2004).

What a wonderful gift to be "quick to observe." It allows us to learn from others' experiences and gain wisdom more quickly and less painfully. Parents can play a major role in helping their children learn through observation. This can be accomplished in dinner-time conversations, in experiences shared in family gatherings, in discussions, during one-on-one outings, in working together, and in any other setting where parents and children can have meaningful interactions. Note that what God is interested in having us learn—the knowledge of good and evil, right and wrong—is *not* being discussed in our modern society *outside the home.*

It is not a serious exaggeration to say that it has become politically incorrect in contemporary American society to speak publicly of standards of morality. Right and wrong are made relative by those who need to rationalize their behavior. We are observing the circumstances described in the scriptures when Isaiah said: "Woe unto them that call evil good, and good evil; that put darkness for light, and light for darkness. . . . Woe unto them that are wise in their own eyes, and prudent in their own sight!" (Isaiah 5:20–21).

Agency and Efficiency

Being "quick to observe" in a trial-and-error envionment has interesting implications concerning time, agency, and efficiency.

Agency on its surface would appear to be a seriously inefficient plan. The devil's plan would have involved much less wasted time and effort compared to the agency-based trial-and-error experience we have in mortality. But this experience is effective to accomplish the purpose of the Lord, which is to bring to pass the "immortality and eternal life of man" (Moses 1:39). The devil's plan, by contrast, was focused primarily on benefiting the devil. His plan was designed to have provided him, personally, with the glory associated with efficiently forcing everyone to obey God's law. But every other individual living under the plan would have sacrificed his own potential to the devil's selfish design. God's plan will bring glory not only to God, but to all of His children who patiently and faithfully follow the plan.

The inefficiency of agency can be attributed to the fact that most of our Father's children expend their efforts in learning by study instead of learning by faith. Learning by study requires that a significant amount of time be devoted to an investigation, by trial and error, of all processes and possible outcomes. God must have known that the gift of agency would be used by His children to explore all available options. Indeed, it is truly amazing that God is willing to tolerate all the trouble and misery caused as the human family applies the headstrong, willful use of agency to explore the whole catalogue of possible experiences. It is impossible to contemplate all the innocent paths, let alone all the deliberately evil roads, that have been explored in the exercise of agency.

Gratefully, our Heavenly Father has the patience that His seemingly inefficient plan requires. I am reminded of a story that Elder Loren Dunn told about his father. Elder Dunn's family lived in Tooele, Utah, and had some property on which they raised cattle. Elder Dunn's father put Loren and his brothers in charge of the fences, the pasture, and the feeding and tending of the cattle. A well-meaning neighbor often commented on the shortcomings and inefficiencies of Father Dunn's cattle-raising operation. One day, after another critical comment, Father Dunn said to the neighbor, "Jim, you don't understand. You see, I'm raising boys and not cows" ("Our Precious Families," *Ensign,* November 1974, 11).

So it is with our Heavenly Father. His plan for the exaltation of His daughters and sons may not appear on the surface to be a very efficient operation. But it is effective in accomplishing His work and bringing to His children the intended blessings. We should be grateful that in the Lord's economy, efficiency is not necessarily the driving force. We would do well to remember that concept as we deal with agency issues in our own parenting.

It is unclear how much to worry about the inefficiency of agency and learning by trial and error. Yes, it is an inefficient process, but how much does it matter? Efficiency is essentially a measure of time. One person or process is more efficient than another if the same amount of work is accomplished in less time or if more work is completed in the same amount of time. But in God's economy, how important is time? He is eternal and His work is everlasting. If, for God, time is not a scarce resource, does it matter how long it takes to accomplish His work?

A parable that seems to support this idea is the parable of the laborers for hire (Matthew 20:1–16). The Savior likened the kingdom of heaven to a householder who hired laborers in the first, third, sixth, ninth, and eleventh hours of the day. Each was paid a penny, regardless of the hour hired or how long he worked. Those who had "borne the burden and heat of the day" (Matthew 20:12) complained that they had not been fairly treated. In other words, they argued in favor of remuneration based on efficiency or output per unit of time. The householder's reply was, "Friend, I do thee no wrong; didst not thou agree with me for a penny? Take that thine is, and go thy way. I will give unto this last, even as unto thee. Is it not lawful for me to do what I will with mine own? Is thine eye evil, because I am good?" Then the Savior concluded the parable by saying, "So the last shall be first, and the first last: for many be called, but few chosen" (Matthew 20:13–16).

The message seems to be that efficiency is not necessarily important in the Lord's economy. By contrast, consider Alma's exhortation to "not procrastinate the day of your repentance" (Alma 13:27). And Samuel the Lamanite exclaims in strong terms, "But behold your days of probation are past; ye have procrastinated the day of your salvation until it is everlastingly too late" (Helaman 13:38).

So time does matter. For God, time may be limitless, but we as individuals do not have an unlimited amount of time to learn the principles of the gospel through inefficient trial-and-error methods. Indeed, there are at least two problems with agency and time. The first and most serious is that using agency to learn by study or trial and error does not have a certain outcome. In other words, the trial-and-error approach does not guarantee a solution in a fixed amount of time. There are so many possibilities to test, so many roads to travel, so many trials to experience that one may run out of time before finding the way. Countless souls are lost when the "days of probation are past" (Helaman 13:38). So trial-and-error agency is both inefficient and uncertain. It is not only time consuming but also has a potentially high probability of failure. How blessed are those who can learn by faith. Learning by faith to keep the commandments is both more efficient and more certain.

The second problem with agency and time has to do with opportunity cost. Learning by trial and error can take up so much time that we lose the opportunity to help others. Eliminating the time, energy, and resources spent in repentance makes it possible to be involved in blessing other lives. If we are to be judged by our good works, the sooner we learn certain principles, the sooner we can be about doing those good works.

A Time-Saving Shortcut

It is possible in several ways to shortcut the passage of time required to gain wisdom. The first way is to have available, on any given process, a cross section of data instead of a time series. A time series of data reflects the accumulation of many observations by one person over time. A cross section of data is one in which many persons have one observation each. A cross section of data could be accumulated by an observer who could look in short order at a process and its outcomes. For example, a judge might on a given day see enough cases of theft that all the outcomes and likelihoods would be observed in a very short period of time.

Researchers in sociology, economics, and political science use both time series and cross-sectional data to discover "truths" about their individual disciplines. Historians use mostly time-series data, but they also observe different civilizations at the same time (cross-sectional data) and try to draw lessons about the behavior of mankind. Careful and unbiased professionals make useful contributions to our understanding of the world in which we live. Curiously enough, however, the academic study of a process does not always result in the wise personal behavior of the researcher.

In general, this process of choosing alternative behaviors and observing the outcomes is what is meant by "learning by study." It includes learning by our own experience to know good from evil. It is how God intended us to gain wisdom and become as the gods. Elder Neal A. Maxwell described mortality as a laboratory in which we perform experiments (see *We Will Prove Them Herewith* [Salt Lake City: Deseret Book, 1982], 16).

None of this unfolding of God's plan would be possible without two salient features of the plan. First, the plan depends on agency and its associated uncertainty, which set up laboratory-type conditions for learning. An environment of determination in which every outcome was known in advance would not work. Agency and uncertainty are essential elements in the plan of God.

The second feature is consistent with the first. For agency, uncertainty, and failed experiments to be acceptable in an eternal perspective, there must be a mechanism that minimizes the cost of failure and provides an incentive for continued learning by study. That mechanism, of course, is the atonement, which provides forgiveness for sincere individuals who repent and call on the atoning blood of Christ to pay the penalty for sins committed in the process of gaining wisdom.

We must know that in the process of learning through experience God will not be mocked. We cannot knowingly make foolish choice after foolish choice, hoping that lip-service repentance will keep us from personally paying the price of our mistakes. We cannot knowingly choose to sin in order to "experience" all that life has to offer. We cannot live a riotous life of immorality, dishonesty, and deceit and hope that in the last days before our death we can somehow avoid eternal consequences.

To summarize, God has given the gift of agency and allows it to be exercised in an earthly setting characterized by uncertainty. Learning by study or observation is one way to gain experience and the wisdom God intended us to gain during our mortal probation. We can validate principles of the gospel through our own choices and through observing the choices made by others. Mistakes made can be forgiven and the penalty paid by the atoning sacrifice of Christ.

CHAPTER TEN

Agency and Learning by Faith

NOAH, HOW LONG can you tread water?" is a line from the hilarious monologue performed by the comedian Bill Cosby as he imagines the Lord speaking to a reluctant Noah. I love the story of Noah. It is one we are all familiar with. But I have overlooked for all these years what I now consider to be one of the most important lessons to be learned from his extraordinary experience. Let me explain.

Suppose I were to ask you to guess Noah's age at the time he started building the ark. Without looking it up in the Bible, what would you answer? Most members of the Church guess he was fairly old, maybe 100 or 200 years, and some guess higher. The answer is that he was 595 years old when he began his boat-building project. My initial reaction when I focused on his age was, "Good grief, it can't be easy to swing a hammer and round up tigers when you are hobbling along on a cane." On further study

I found that he lived another 305 years after starting to build the ark, finally dying at the age of 900. Clearly we can't compare how he felt at 595 to how we feel at 65 or 70 years old. Something was definitely different then, compared to the current realities we face with the aging process. Nevertheless, his age of 595 years allows us to focus on one of the most interesting and useful insights to be gained from his remarkable story.

To make the point, let's consider for a moment the modern notion of evaluating the risk of flooding with respect to a potential building site. Generally speaking, those charged with approving building sites make their decision by examining data from past years. If actual data is unavailable, they may turn to "old timers" who have personal experience with floods in the area. The data or experience is usually communicated in terms of the highest watermark in the past 10 or 50 or 100 years. The idea is that only those sites that lie above a reasonably high waterline will be approved. If you keep track of the local experience with flood water and build on land that lies above the highest watermark that has been experienced in the last 100 years, you've been a reasonable risk manager. Indeed, you have been *learning by study*.

A homeowner who builds above the 100-year flood line should feel comfortable and safe. In addition, in such circumstances flood insurance is usually readily available and reasonably priced. However, a very risk-averse homeowner might consult local flood-level records and decide to build above a line representing 200 years of experience instead of just 100 years. And if 200 years is better, why not look at the 300-year experience record? At some point a person has to say that any additional prudence is unwarranted and unnecessary.

Now let us return to Noah. Noah had lived 595 years! He had personally experienced six centuries and could have drawn six lines on the hillside, each of which represented a 100-year flood level.

He could look at the six lines and point to the highest of the six as the 600-year high watermark! During each of the six previous 100-year high water times, he had taken his family, moved to high ground, and sat on the hillside until the water went down. Perhaps he had decided to move his house; perhaps he concluded that it wasn't worth the effort.

The point is, here is a man with a whole lot of experience with high water—600 years worth. He had been diligently *learning by study*. And so when the Lord said to him, Noah, you need to build an ark, what could he easily have said? You can almost imagine him saying, "Lord, I've lived 595 years in this same house. And over there on the hillside I've kept track of the high-water marks. You see, Lord, there are six lines, each representing the highest the water rose in 100 years. The highest mark, you see it right there, is only halfway up that hill. I remember that flood well. Sister Noah and I took the children and all the animals and our 72-hour kits and spent three days camping on the hillside. The kids loved it! The water went down and we were back in our house in a week. The insurance adjuster came by and settled up our claim. Lord, I'm an experienced man. I'm a prudent man. I've experienced the highest water in 595 years. Why on earth would I need an ark?"

That's what Noah could have said, but of course he didn't! And that has become for me the really exciting and inspiring part of the story. Noah was willing to allow learning by faith to trump learning by study and experience. It didn't matter that he had 595 years of experience with floods. It didn't matter that everyone else in the community who also had experience probably thought he was a fool. It didn't matter that he'd never built an ark or that he'd have to get up every morning for five years and pound nails—or that he'd be doing it at age 595, 596, 597, 598, and 599.

What obviously mattered to Noah was his faith in the Lord. His faith was more powerful than his experience. Noah correctly answered the following question: When faced with uncertainty, who should you believe, yourself (that is, your own experience) or the Lord? Noah understood that the purpose of life is *not* to gain enough experience that faith is not necessary.

Noah's faith is referenced in the book of Hebrews. We read, "By faith Noah, being warned of God of *things not seen as yet,* moved with fear, prepared an ark to the saving of his house" (Hebrews 11:7; emphasis added). No amount of experience, as valuable as it was, could have prepared Noah for "things not seen as yet." Noah was willing, despite his 595 years of experience, to take counsel from the Lord and learn by faith. The great lesson to be learned from Noah and from a host of other examples in the scriptures is to learn "*also by faith.*"

Uncertainty and Faith

In chapter nine we introduced a diagram to accompany the spiritual injunction to "seek learning, even by study and also by faith" (D&C 88:118). That diagram is reproduced as figure 10–1.

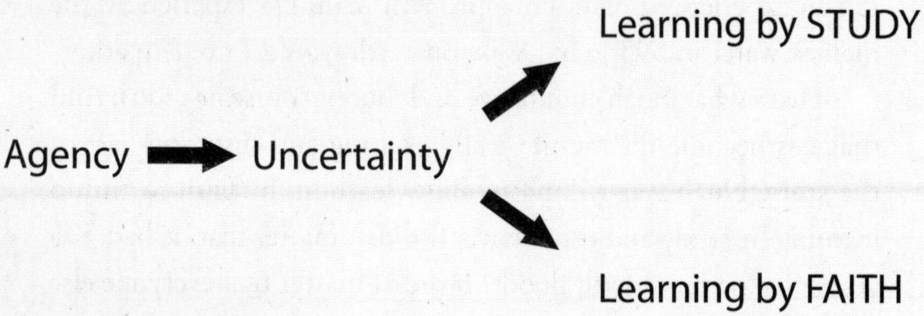

Learning by STUDY

Agency ➡ Uncertainty

Learning by FAITH

Figure 10–1

We learned in chapter nine that agency opens the door and produces a set of conditions under which we can learn by study and careful observation. Through our study and analysis of processes and outcomes, we can discover correct principles.

In the same way that agency opens the door to learning by study and observation, it also opens the door to learning by faith. No faith is required in a certain or deterministic environment where everything is known and all processes have only one outcome. By giving us the gift of agency in a world of uncertainty, God also gave us the opportunity to exercise faith and choose whether or not to believe in His pronouncements.

Faith is not developed in an environment of certainty but in an environment of uncertainty. The contacting that missionaries are encouraged to do in the mission field is a good illustration of this notion. We often talked with our missionaries about their contacting experiences and the different ways in which people responded to their message. Sometimes missionaries admitted to being a wee bit discouraged when they had talked to twenty-five or thirty people in a row without finding a single one who was interested. Occasionally, when pressed, they admitted that it was maybe more like fifty or sixty people in a row and that they were more than just a little discouraged.

I asked them to tell me what happened next. What did they do? They explained that something strange often happened. After being rejected fifty times in a row they then often found five people in a row who were eager to hear their message. They concluded they just had to "have the faith to persevere." In subsequent conversations with discouraged missionaries, I would remind them that missionary work was "lumpy" and that the lumps came in different sizes. I meant by that that they might have a long or short series of rejections followed by a short or long series of acceptances and that such a pattern was just part of the work.

Once they experienced both parts of the lumpiness, they would have learned that the key to success was to have the faith to persevere.

What I labeled for the missionaries as *lumpiness* illustrates the role that uncertainty plays in the development of faith. Uncertainty demonstrates the randomness in the outcomes we experience with most processes in life. One day in a discussion with a missionary about the problem of lumpiness, or random outcomes, I observed that it really might be more encouraging if the work wasn't so lumpy. Wouldn't it be nice, I said, if instead of having an unknown number of rejections in a row, followed by an unknown number of acceptances, you could just automatically have exactly every tenth person accept to hear the message? The missionary paused for a moment and then said, "President, where would be the faith in that?" Where, indeed, I thought!

Agency and uncertainty create an environment of unpredictability. We can best negotiate that environment by exercising faith in the pronouncements of God.

The advantages to learning by faith are enormous. If we choose to exercise our agency and by faith accept the challenge to keep the commandments of God, we can learn, grow, and progress in all the ways that God intended. We can eliminate or reduce the serious problems we create for ourselves in the school of hard knocks by being willing to learn by faith. But will we thereby avoid all the sorrow and heartaches of this life? No, because we will always be affected by the choices made by others.

Exercising our agency to learn by faith is not unique to our earthly estate. God's children have always had the option to learn by faith—and they always will have—because agency is a principle that operates in all three states of our experience: premortal, mortal, and postmortal.

In our premortal existence it was necessary to have faith in the plan of redemption proposed by God and Christ. It was necessary to have faith that Christ would fulfill His role in the plan. There was enough uncertainty in the outcome, owing to agency, that only two-thirds of the hosts of heaven were willing to commit to the plan. The devil played on fear, the opposite of faith, to cause one-third of our Father's children to oppose His plan and follow the adversary.

Clearly faith is also at work in our mortal state. It requires faith to keep commandments without having first personally experienced the consequences. It requires faith, when commandments are broken, to repent and believe in the power of the atonement to satisfy the demands of justice. It requires faith to understand how the Savior can comfort those whose sorrow and anguish are caused by the misuse of agency by others.

Faith will be at work in the postmortal experience as well. Evidence is provided by the vision opened to Joseph F. Smith and recorded in Doctrine and Covenants 138.

> And the chosen messengers went forth to declare the acceptable day of the Lord and proclaim liberty to the captives who were bound, even unto all who would repent of their sins and receive the gospel.
>
> Thus was the gospel preached to those who had died in their sins, without a knowledge of the truth, or in transgression, having rejected the prophets.
>
> *These were taught faith in God,* repentance from sin, vicarious baptism for the remission of sins, the gift of the Holy Ghost by the laying on of hands,
>
> And all other principles of the gospel that were necessary for them to know in order to qualify themselves that they might be judged according to men in the flesh, but

live according to God in the spirit. (D&C 138:31–34; emphasis added)

When verse 33 states that "*these were taught faith in God,*" it means that those who had died without a knowledge of the plan of redemption and the role of the Savior had to be taught the principles of faith—and, more important, they had to exercise agency and faith in order to make future progress.

We can choose to believe and develop faith, or we can choose not to believe and have no faith. The role of agency in developing faith is explained by Moroni in the book of Ether. There he explains that "faith is things which are hoped for and not seen" and that "ye receive no witness until after the trial of your faith" (Ether 12:6). A trial in this context is best thought of as a *test*. So Moroni is saying that faith is developed by having enough hope that you choose (exercise agency) to put something to the test.

Alma makes a similar point in his well-known discourse on faith. He invites his listeners to "awake and arouse your faculties, *even to an experiment* upon my words" (Alma 32:27; emphasis added). Alma uses the word *experiment* to convey the idea that one who wishes to develop faith must exercise agency and take some action to test or experiment upon the word.

It is important for all who teach the gospel—parents, priesthood and auxiliary leaders, teachers in classrooms, and missionaries—to understand the process that leads to faith and to emphasize the role that agency plays in that process. The first step in helping others develop faith is to declare the word to them. That means that the teacher must teach or explain a principle of the gospel. The new missionary training book, *Preach My Gospel,* is marvelous in helping not only missionaries but any gospel teacher learn principles of the gospel that they can declare and bear witness to in their own words.

The second step is to teach those who would have faith that they also must have hope, as pointed out by Moroni. Or, as suggested by Alma, they must at least have a "desire to believe" (Alma 32:27) that the principle being taught is true. Hope and desire can be built in others by promising blessings that can be found in the scriptures.

Then comes the critical step. It is necessary for those being taught *to exercise agency* and to act on their hope or desire by doing something to begin putting the declared principle to the test. Such actions could include reading, praying, and attending meetings, among others. But these actions have to be invited, not coerced. Once the invitation is accepted and a commitment made to take a particular action, gospel teachers can follow up the commitment with encouragement.

Those being taught gospel principles by this process are exercising agency and putting Moroni's teachings to the test. If they are sincere in their desires and actions and have clearly understood the principle being taught, they will receive the witness spoken of by Moroni. They will believe the principle is true and will be prepared to be taught another principle that can be tested or tried in the same manner.

The development of faith is the same for mature Latter-day Saints as it is for nonmembers who wish to investigate the teachings of the Church. Developing faith in the principles of the gospel requires us to hope they are true, put them to the test by living them, and then receive a witness of their truthfulness as we choose to exercise agency.

President Hinckley made this point beautifully to the Saints in Paris, France, when he said, "I plead with you, my brothers and sisters, that if you have any doubt concerning any doctrine of this Church, that you put it to the test. Try it. Live the principle. Get on your knees and pray about it, and God will bless you with a knowledge of the truth of this work" ("Inspirational Thoughts," *Ensign,* September 2007, 6).

This is the essence of learning by faith: learning true principles in the Lord's way. The role of agency in the process of learning "also by faith" is described by Elder David A. Bednar:

> A learner exercising agency by acting in accordance with correct principles opens his or her heart to the Holy Ghost and invites His teaching, testifying power, and confirming witness. Learning by faith requires spiritual, mental, and physical exertion and not just passive reception. It is in the sincerity and consistency of our faith-inspired action that we indicate to our Heavenly Father and His Son, Jesus Christ, our willingness to learn and receive instruction from the Holy Ghost. *Thus, learning by faith involves the exercise of moral agency to act upon the assurance of things hoped for and invites the evidence of things not seen from the only true teacher, the Spirit of the Lord.* ("Seek Learning by Faith," *Ensign,* September 2007, 64; emphasis added)

The Lord is most concerned that we learn principles pertaining to good and evil or right and wrong. We can learn these principles by our own trial and error, meaning by our own experience. We can also learn them by faith. The combination of learning by study and also by faith is designed to bring us to the state of wisdom, judgment, and knowledge of good and evil envisioned by Adam and Eve when they partook of the fruit in the Garden of Eden.

A certain, or deterministic, plan would make it impossible to learn either by study or by faith. Learning by trial and error, by our own experience, would not be possible because we could not choose to test any action and examine the outcome. Learning by faith would not be possible because we could never choose to test or experiment on the word of God. Our development would be arrested, and there would be no hope that we could ever become like God. How grateful we should be that God gave the gift of agency and that we chose to take it.

CHAPTER ELEVEN

Agency, the Earth, and Strict Obedience

A S MY WIFE AND I were raising our seven sons, one issue that continually occupied a priority position on our family home evening agenda was the chaos we observed in the boys' bedrooms. Clothes were strewn everywhere, beds were unmade, sweat-drenched uniforms stood by themselves in the corners, balls of all sizes and shapes were scattered around, and total disarray was the daily order. We cajoled, we pleaded, we threatened, and we bribed; in short, we tried all the methods we could think of to bring order out of chaos. Nothing seemed to work, and so we resorted to the tried-and-true adage—out of sight, out of mind—and we told the boys to please just keep their bedroom doors closed.

One day Margaret, the unfailing optimist, sat down with one of the boys in a one-on-one setting and reviewed the merits of cleanliness and order. That day she focused on making the bed. She helped him make it, as she had done dozens of times before.

But that day, instead of moving on to the rest of the mess, she held him tight, told him how much she loved him, and explained what a blessing it would be to her if he would just be obedient and make his bed every day.

She didn't think much more about it until several months later. Then it dawned on her that every time in recent memory she'd checked, that boy's bed was made. I explained to her about holes in the space-time continuum that would explain the miraculous self-making bed. I secretly supposed the boy had taken to sleeping on top of the bed so he wouldn't have to bother with remaking it every day. We checked out that theory by looking in on him one night and found him under the covers and between the sheets as he ought to have been. There were only two explanations to our observation that the bed was always made: either we really had discovered a new natural law—the amazing self-making bed—or the boy was being strictly obedient and making his bed every day without fail. Either way, the outcome was the same: the bed was always made.

Now the point of the story is this: to observers, the outcome through strict obedience was indistinguishable from that through the "new natural law of the self-making bed." We could clearly observe the outcome but could not necessarily know the mechanism by which the outcome was achieved. With that story in mind, let us consider how the concept of agency may suggest something about the workings of the earth.

In previous chapters we have discussed the concept of how agency creates an environment of uncertainty that is contrasted to a certain, or deterministic, system. I referred to gravity as an example of a deterministic phenomenon: objects always fall down, never up or sideways. The laws that govern the physical organization of the earth seem to be deterministic, at least within the range of observation that we normally experience. Sir Isaac Newton was a scientist who focused his attention on observing the physical processes of the earth. He proposed a set of laws that describes the workings of nature. To an observer on earth, these "laws of nature" appear to yield outcomes that are fixed and immutable. But is it possible that these same observations could be the result of a process involving strict obedience?

Let's now investigate a hypothesis concerning agency and the earth. We will not have sufficient data to prove or disprove it, but the hope is that our investigation will add to our understanding of agency. At the least, we will have some interesting questions for further discussion. Our hypothesis is that the earth has agency and is strictly obedient.

In the book of Moses we read the fascinating account of the Lord's interaction with Enoch. Moses 6 and 7 chronicles the vision he was given and the conversations of the Lord with Enoch. Late in chapter 7 we read, "And it came to pass that Enoch looked upon the earth; and *he heard a voice from the bowels thereof,* saying: Wo, wo is me, the mother of men; I am pained, I am weary, because of the wickedness of my children. When shall I rest, and be cleansed from the filthiness which is gone forth out of me? When will my Creator sanctify me, that I may rest, and righteousness for a season abide upon my face?" (Moses 7:48; emphasis added). While this may be poetic license or literary anthropomorphizing (ascribing human attributes to something that is not human), let us proceed as if it were literally the voice of the earth.

One interesting implication of Enoch's hearing the voice of the earth is that somehow the earth is in a state that we normally speak of as being alive. In other words, it is not an inanimate object but is animated by a living spirit. The earth seems to experience pain and weariness, which are traits or emotions attributed to a living entity. It is somehow conscious of the difference between wickedness and righteousness and petitions the Creator for righteousness and rest. In other words, the earth exhibits not only self-awareness but also *moral awareness.*

In Moses 7:49, we read that "Enoch heard the earth mourn," implying again that it was alive. In Doctrine and Covenants 123:7 the Prophet Joseph says, "The whole earth groans under the weight of its iniquity." It is not entirely clear in what manner the earth is "alive." If the earth as a whole entity can experience pain and weariness and differentiates between wickedness and righteousness, we might wonder about the subparts or constituent elements that make up the earth. Are the mountains alive? Is there some manner in which the seas and trees can be considered to be conscious in the same way that man is conscious?

The book of Abraham uses fascinating language to describe the creation of the earth. Abraham 4:1 explains that the Gods (plural) organized and formed (not created) the heavens and the earth. The fact that multiple Gods were involved and that the earth was not created but organized is doctrine that is well known and expounded upon (F. Kent Nielsen and Stephen D. Ricks, "Creation, Creation Accounts," in Daniel H. Ludlow, ed., *Encyclopedia of Mormonism,* 4 vols. [New York: Macmillan, 1992], 1:340–43).

But I would like to focus attention on the phrases that end nine verses in chapter four, beginning with verses 7 and 9, which include the words *"it was so, even as they ordered"* (Abraham 4:7) and *"it was so as they ordered"* (verse 9). The word *ordered* in the two verses could be used in the military sense of an order being given and obeyed. *Ordered* could also mean that things were put in proper sequence or relationship to one another.

However, the next verses are much more to the point. Verse 10 concludes with the phrase, *"and the Gods saw that they were obeyed."* In other words, orders were given and were followed or obeyed. Verses 11 and 12 again repeat the words *ordered* and *obeyed.*

It is verse 18, where both the words *ordered* and *obeyed* are employed together, that seems to fully confirm what is implied in the previous verses. Verse 18 reads, *"And the Gods watched those things which they had ordered until they obeyed."*

The intriguing implication of these verses is that the things being watched had a choice to obey or not to obey. In other words, one way to interpret the language found in the verses is that the things being watched had some form of agency. Yet the things being watched over were those we generally think of as being inanimate. The things that "obeyed" were the waters (verses 7, 9); the dry land (verse 9); the grass, herb, and trees (verse 12); the days and nights; and the greater and lesser lights (verses 13–18).

The "moving creatures that have life," including the fowls and whales, are the subject of verses 20 and 21. Verse 21 then concludes with the phrase, "And the Gods saw that *they would be obeyed, and that their plan was good"* (emphasis added). The cattle, beasts, and creeping things of the earth are spoken of in verses 24 and 25, and yet again *"the Gods saw they would obey."*

The ninth and final phrase concerning obedience is found in Abraham 4:31. It reads: "And the Gods said: We will do everything that we have said, and organize them; and behold, *they shall be very obedient"* (emphasis added). This is a wonderful concluding phrase because the words "very obedient" describe the kind of strict adherence that is indistinguishable from a deterministic system.

What an interesting idea! Is it possible that the laws of Newtonian physics that describe much of our observable physical environment are simply a reflection of strict obedience by the various constituent parts of the earth that are exercising agency? Could it be that the mechanism by which the earth was formed and organized is obedience to an order or a verbal request from the Gods?

In Psalms we read, "By the word of the Lord were the heavens made; and all the host of them by the breath of his mouth" (Psalm 33:6). And further, "For he spake, and it was done; *he commanded, and it stood fast*" (Psalm 33:9; emphasis added). The heavens were made by speaking ("by the word of the Lord") and "stood fast" or became certain and unvarying by His command. Standing fast is a good description of deterministic systems and also of the notion of being "very obedient."

Moving things around requires power. Tables and chairs can be moved by a husband and wife. Cars are powered by engines that generate two hundred or three hundred horsepower. Diesel locomotives and oceangoing ships must be moved by engines that generate thousands of horsepower. It is entirely conceivable that the voice of an infinite, omnipotent God could vibrate with enough raw power to move the earth and its mountains and seas. Alternatively, by His command, the hosts of heaven could begin pulling and pushing until the desired result was achieved. But could it be that He spake and whatever was to be acted upon "obeyed" and moved itself?

Support for this interesting idea is found in the writings of Elder John A. Widtsoe and his discussion of the teachings of the Prophet Joseph Smith. He wrote:

> Associated with matter-energy was the implication in Joseph Smith's teachings that *the energy in the universe is a form of intelligence;* that is, in a manner not fully understood by man, some form of life resides in all matter, though of an order wholly different from the organized intelligence of men or higher living things. Hence, everything in the universe is alive. The differences among rock,

plant, beast, and man are due to the amount and organization of the life element. Confirming this view, the Prophet in a revelation said: "The earth . . . shall be sanctified; yea, notwithstanding it shall die, it shall be quickened again, and shall abide the power by which it is quickened." (D&C 88:25–26)

That implies clearly that the earth is a living organism. . . .

We live then in a living universe which in all its component parts is intelligent. (John A. Widtsoe, *Joseph Smith: Seeker After Truth, Prophet of God* [Salt Lake City: Bookcraft, 1957], 149–50)

A wonderful little vignette is found in the book of Helaman. In chapter 12, Mormon is interjecting into the record his observations about the nature of men. By this time in the record he has read and written about nearly six hundred years of Nephite history and has documented over and over the pride cycle he has observed. His words are very much in the form of a lament, which he begins by pointing out "the unsteadiness of the hearts of the children of men" (Helaman 12:1). He explains how much the Lord does for His people, which they quickly forget when they become prosperous. He talks about their foolishness and pride and how quick they are to do iniquity. He then says, "Behold, they do not desire that the Lord their God, who hath created them, should rule and reign over them; notwithstanding his great goodness and his mercy towards them, they do set at naught his counsels, and they will not that he should be their guide" (Helaman 12:6).

Mormon's lament is that men will not be obedient. They exercise their agency in setting "*at naught his counsels*" and refuse to be directed or guided by the Lord. He continues, "O how great is the nothingness of the children of men; yea, even they are less than the dust of the earth" (Helaman 12:7). In his frustration he is saying, to put it colloquially, that men are *dumber than dirt*. Men are just not willing to obey. By contrast he explains, "For behold, the dust of the earth moveth hither and thither, to the dividing asunder, *at the command* of our great and everlasting God. Yea, behold *at his voice* do the hills and the mountains tremble and quake. And by the *power of his voice* they are broken up, and become smooth, yea, even like unto a valley" (Helaman 12:8–10; emphasis added).

Mormon is clearly contrasting the disobedience of man to the obedience of something so lowly and insignificant as the dust of the earth. His wonderment is that if dirt will hearken to the voice of the Lord and be obedient to His command, why will not man respond in the same manner? He continues his argument in verses 13 through 17: "Yea, and if he say unto the earth—Move—it is moved" (Helaman 12:13). Notice that even the punctuation is chosen to convey the notion of a command that is obeyed. *Move* is in the imperative tense meaning you-move. It is written with a capital *M* and set between two dashes as would be done with a direct quotation.

"Yea, if he say unto the earth—Thou shalt go back, that it lengthen out the day for many hours—it is done; and thus, *according to his word* the earth goeth back, and it appeareth unto man that the sun standeth still; yea, and behold, this is so; for surely it is the earth that moveth and not the sun" (Helaman 12:14–15; emphasis added).

As an aside, it is impressive to note that Mormon had a correct understanding of celestial mechanics, because he realized the earth revolves around the sun and not vice versa.

"And behold, also, if he say unto the waters of the great deep—Be thou dried up—it is done.

"Behold, if he say unto this mountain—Be thou raised up,

and come over and fall upon that city, that it be buried up—behold it is done" (Helaman 12:16–17).

Mormon concludes his lament by pointing out that the disobedience of man will not go unpunished:

> And behold, if the Lord shall say unto a man—Because of thine iniquities, thou shalt be accursed forever—it shall be done.
>
> And if the Lord shall say—Because of thine iniquities thou shalt be cut off from my presence—he will cause that it shall be so.
>
> And wo unto him to whom he shall say this, for it shall be unto him that will do iniquity, and he cannot be saved; therefore, for this cause, that men might be saved, hath repentance been declared. (Helaman 12:20–22)

Finally, Mormon makes the point that he has been leading up to. He says, "Blessed are they who will repent and hearken unto the voice of the Lord their God; for these are they that shall be saved" (Helaman 12:23). His point is that we must be smart enough to obey. Be like the dust of the earth and be obedient. Do not commit iniquity. Exercise moral agency and choose righteousness rather than wickedness.

In the end, Mormon's lament is simple. The dust of the earth can obey—why can't you? In pondering these notions I penned some verses that try to capture the obedience of the earth and the disobedience of man.

Be Wise, O Man

O thou, the Word who made all things,
How didst thou fill the void?
Do heavens, earth, and seas recall

Thy power on them employed?

Was each by force assigned a part

Through strength and might and will?

And pushed and pulled into a place

That would thy plan fulfill?

Or were the agents simply asked

If they would but obey

And honor the atoning Son

Until the judgment day?

O man who from the dust was formed

And given the gift of will,

A veil is drawn across thine eyes;

Heaven's voice to thee is still.

Yet earth has chosen to obey.

The seas and mountains hear;

Canst thou not find it in thy heart

To lend a listening ear?

O foolish man, be wise as dust;

Stand fast in heaven's way.

And with the earth be sanctified

Upon the judgment day.

Why Does the Dust Obey?

The question might be asked, Why do the mountains, seas, trees, and even the dust obey? If they indeed have agency and can exercise it, why do they choose to be very obedient? One explanation may have to do with the veil that was drawn over our consciousness as part of our earthly experience. Perhaps the earth and its constituent elements do not have any such veil. The Doctrine and Covenants describes how men will react when that veil is lifted:

And this shall be the sound of his trump, saying to all people, both in heaven and in earth, . . . for every ear shall hear it, and every knee shall bow, and every tongue shall confess, while they hear the sound of the trump, saying: Fear God, and give glory to him who sitteth upon the throne, forever and ever. (D&C 88:104)

The bowing of knee and confessing of tongue will not come by force but will be a voluntary action evoked by the revealing of the glory and majesty of God. Perhaps that glory and majesty are not hidden to the earth. The omnipotence of God; the infinite, atoning sacrifice of Christ; the love of the Father and the Son may be continually before the earth. The response of the earth to that knowledge and understanding is to be obedient. It is to remain obedient to the command that it was given when the earth was formed and organized. In the same way that obedient children honor the love, sacrifice, and teaching of their parents, an obedient earth honors the love and sacrifice of the Son of God who organized it.

The veil drawn over our eyes serves to allow us to obtain, develop, and strengthen our faith through exercising agency. The exactness of the earth's obedience assists us in that process. Consider how difficult our existence would be if there were not some measure of stability in our physical environment. The sun rises and sets on a regular basis, we walk on solid ground, and the seasons come and go. The regularity of the physical laws provides a more or less stable environment in which to exercise moral agency. There is enough certainty in our surroundings that our hearts do not fail us and enough uncertainty that we learn to exercise faith in God and in the wisdom of keeping His commandments.

The scriptures speak of a time when "all things shall be in commotion; and surely, men's hearts shall fail them" (D&C 88:91).

This is a condition that will exist just before the Second Coming of the Lord. We read in Doctrine and Covenants 88:87: "For not many days hence and the earth shall tremble and reel to and fro as a drunken man; and the sun shall hide his face, and shall refuse to give light; and the moon shall be bathed in blood; and the stars shall become exceedingly angry, and shall cast themselves down as a fig that falleth from off a fig-tree."

Notice that the language in the verse speaks of the sun hiding and refusing to give light and the stars becoming angry and casting themselves down. The language may well be literary, but the behavior described is consistent with the exercise of agency.

Verses 89 and 90 continue with this language:

> For after your testimony cometh the testimony of earthquakes, that shall cause groanings in the midst of *her* [the earth], and men shall fall upon the ground and shall not be able to stand.
>
> And also cometh the testimony of the voice of thunderings, and the voice of lightnings, and the voice of tempests, and the voice of the waves of the sea heaving themselves beyond their bounds. (Emphasis added)

The language implies that agency is being exercised by earthquakes, lightnings, tempests, and the waves of the sea as their voices provide testimony.

After describing these unusual phenomenon, the scriptures say, "And all things shall be in commotion; and surely, men's hearts shall fail them; for fear shall come upon all people" (D&C 88:91).

When the Lord's Second Coming is imminent, the time for developing faith is past. The stable physical environment that has been the norm for thousands of years has allowed men to focus, if they so choose, on developing faith, exercising moral agency, and gaining the wisdom and judgment God intended. In the end, having all things in commotion will bring fear and failed hearts. The interruptions of the certainty, the determination, and standing fast that has characterized the earth will signal the end of man's probationary state.

The vocal and physical testimony of the earth at the last day is in contrast to its silent acquiescence to all that has gone on prior to that time. Apparently the earth is conscious of the difference between wickedness and righteousness. As referenced earlier in the chapter, Enoch heard the voice of the earth mourning over the wickedness and filthiness that existed on it and wished to know when it would be able to rest. But while conscious of wickedness and righteousness, it is not allowed, except on rare occasions, to react to that awareness. For example, in deference to the moral agency of man, the earth does not prevent men from waging war, taking innocent lives, committing immorality, or otherwise breaking any of the commandments of God. In general, the earth is not allowed to distinguish between the barley farmer whose crop will be used to produce an alcoholic, Word of Wisdom breaking, drink from one whose crop will be used otherwise. The earth cannot choose to withhold its strength from the tobacco farmer whose crop will be turned into cigarettes or cigars. Many other examples could be cited to illustrate that the earth must remain morally neutral while men learn to exercise moral agency.

The Earth's Obedience

Can the earth or its elements be obedient to a request or command issued by someone other than God? Apparently so, under certain conditions. Moses parted the Red Sea. Joshua commanded the sun to stand still, and "the sun stood still in the midst of heaven, and hasted not to go down about a whole day" (Joshua 10:12–13). (It is likely that this account of the sun standing still was known to Mormon and prompted his editorial comment in Helaman 12:14–15, noted previously in the chapter.) Enoch moved mountains and rivers: "He spake the word of the Lord, and the earth trembled, and the mountains fled, even according to his command; and the rivers of water were turned out of their course" (Moses 7:13). There are numerous other examples of the earth or its elements responding to the command of an authorized servant of the Lord.

The account of Nephi, the son of Helaman, provides a partial insight into some of the conditions that accompany these phenomena. Nephi is told by the Lord that he had with unwearyingness "not sought thine own life, but hast sought my will, and to keep my commandments" (Helaman 10:4). Because of his zealousness in keeping the commandments and seeking the will of the Lord, Nephi was further told, "I will make thee mighty in word and in deed, in faith and in works; yea, even that all things shall be done unto thee according to thy word, *for thou shalt not ask that which is contrary to my will*" (Helaman 10:5; emphasis added).

Because the Lord had such complete confidence in the manner in which Nephi would use his agency, He said to Nephi, "Behold, I give unto you power, that whatsoever ye shall seal on earth shall be sealed in heaven; and whatsoever ye shall loose on earth shall be loosed in heaven; and thus shall ye have power among this people. . . . And if ye shall say unto this mountain, Be thou cast down and become smooth, it shall be done" (Helaman 10:7, 9).

Nephi had demonstrated his complete obedience and desire to do the Lord's will. In return, the Lord gave unto him power to seal in heaven and on earth and also power to command the elements. We are not told the mechanism by which that power would operate. But perhaps the elements were instructed by the Lord to be obedient to Nephi's commands as if they were His own.

Another example of the earth recognizing authorized servants of the Lord is a personal favorite of mine, perhaps because of its decidedly literary character. When I presided over the Switzerland Geneva Mission, I often quoted Isaiah 55 to our missionaries. I was eager for them to realize who they were and what it meant to be ordained, set-apart messengers who were going forth declaring the word of the Lord. The first half of the chapter introduces the notion that salvation is free and comes to those who seek the Lord and call upon Him while He is near. In verses eight and nine, the Lord explains that His thoughts and ways are not like ours but are higher and by implication much more profound.

Then in verses 10 through 12 we read:

> For as the rain cometh down, and the snow from heaven, and returneth not thither, but watereth the earth, and maketh it bring forth and bud, that it may give seed to the sower, and bread to the eater:
>
> So shall my word be that goeth forth out of my mouth: it shall not return unto me void, but it shall accomplish that which I please, and it shall prosper in the thing whereto I sent it.
>
> For ye shall go out with joy, and be led forth with peace: the mountains and the hills shall break forth before you into singing, and all the trees of the field shall clap their hands.

The Lord explains that the rain and snow don't get halfway to the ground and then turn around and go back up into the clouds. They fulfill their purpose of watering the ground and allowing it to bring forth food for man. In the same manner, the word of the Lord carried by His missionaries does "not return unto me void, but it shall accomplish that which I please, and it shall prosper in the thing whereto I sent it." It was helpful to the missionaries to realize that the message they were carrying would fulfill the purposes of the Lord and their labor, no matter how hard, would not be in vain. I wanted them, as verse 12 explains, to "*go out with joy, and be led forth with peace.*" I wanted them to be happy in their labors and to be not afraid.

I told them that, as they walked the beautiful mountains and hills of Switzerland and France, if they listened closely perhaps they could hear the "mountains and hills . . . break forth . . . into singing" and the "trees of the field . . . clap their hands." I wished for them to understand that the mountains, hills, and trees recognized the authorized servants of the Lord. I wanted them to know that the elements of the earth were aware of who they are and the message they carry and most of all who sent them. After all, the word of salvation they carried came from the same Jehovah who organized the earth; it was the same Jehovah that both the earth and the missionaries had chosen to obey.

Of course, Isaiah 55 can be thought of simply as literary imagery designed to inspire and lift our spirits. But could it also be, as we have hypothesized in this chapter, that the elements of the earth are in some way alive and are aware of the servants of the Lord?

A final note. We speak of living things as growing old and passing away or dying. Of the earth Isaiah says, "The earth shall wax old like a garment, and they that dwell therein shall die in like manner" (Isaiah 51:6; 2 Nephi 8:6). Ether prophesied that when the end comes, "the earth *shall pass away.* And there shall be a new heaven and a new earth; and they shall be like unto the old save the old have passed away, and all things have become new" (Ether 13:8–9; emphasis added). And in the Doctrine and Covenants we read:

And the end shall come, and the heaven and the earth shall be consumed and *pass away,* and there shall be a new heaven and a new earth.

For all old things shall pass away, and all things shall become new, even the heaven and the earth, and all the fulness thereof, both men and beasts, the fowls of the air, and the fishes of the sea;

And not one hair, neither mote, shall be lost. (D&C 29:23–25; emphasis added)

The inference of these verses is that the earth will die and then be renewed but be "like unto the old." This is the same kind of language used when we speak of the death and resurrection of individuals, and "not one hair shall be lost." Are the words in the scriptures chosen to describe something that will happen to the earth that will be "like unto" death and resurrection? Can they be taken literally to mean that the earth is alive in the same manner that we are alive and will be renewed or resurrected in a manner similar to all living things?

In latter-day revelation the Lord said, "The earth abideth the law of a celestial kingdom, for it filleth the measure of its creation, and *transgresseth not the law*—Wherefore, it shall be sanctified; yea, notwithstanding it shall die, it shall be quickened again" (D&C 88:25–26; emphasis added).

Here the Lord, in addition to reiterating what is said elsewhere about the earth dying and being quickened again, explains that the earth "transgresseth not the law." How interesting! The earth has been "obedient" and will die but will be renewed and will abide the law of the celestial kingdom. Or, as we read in the tenth article of faith, "the earth will be renewed and receive its paradisiacal glory."

We have come full circle, from Abraham's language of "and

the Gods watched those things which they had ordered until they obeyed" (Abraham 4:18) to the language of the Doctrine and Covenants, "for it filleth the measure of its creation, and transgresseth not the law" (D&C 88:25).

And what of our hypothesis? Is the earth alive and strictly obedient or is it inanimate and not acting but always being acted upon? Are the scriptures to be taken literally, or are we being offered symbolic language to communicate somewhat nebulous concepts?

In either case the message is clear. We as Heavenly Father's children are alive and do have our agency. We are blessed to be alive to act and not just be acted upon. We can choose to be obedient as is the "dust of the earth" and through our obedience inherit the celestial kingdom. We can also fill the measure of our creation in the same manner as will the earth—by not transgressing the law and by being obedient. The measure of our creation is to live with our heavenly parents in the celestial kingdom. The measure of the earth's creation is to be that celestial kingdom on which we live. What a glorious reunion we both can look forward to.

CHAPTER TWELVE

Agency and the Holy Ghost

THE ROLES OF THE Holy Ghost are many and varied. The Holy Ghost is a testifier (Moses 5:9), a revelator (2 Peter 1:21), a comforter (John 14:16–27), a sanctifier (D&C 84:33), a compliance officer (Moses 6:60), and a recorder (Moses 6:61).

This third member of the Godhead does not possess a body but is a personage of spirit, as its name implies. Though a spirit, the Holy Ghost is not without power. The Holy Ghost clearly has the option to be heard and felt in powerful ways, such as occurred on the day of Pentecost. On that occasion those present heard "a sound from heaven as of a rushing mighty wind" and "there appeared unto them cloven tongues like as of fire" (Acts 2:2–3).

But these manifestations of power are the exception rather than the rule. Why are the workings of the Holy Ghost generally so subtle? Consider, for example, the role of the Holy Ghost as testifier. If it is important for an individual to gain a witness of the divinity of the Savior—and it clearly is—why is this process almost without exception totally lacking in physical or outward signs? We do have the notable exceptions of Paul in the New Testament and Alma in the Book of Mormon. But many millions have gained a testimony of the gospel and the role of Christ as Savior and Redeemer through the quieter means of a burning in the bosom (see D&C 9:8) or a still small voice (see 1 Kings 19:12; D&C 85:6).

Is there an explanation for this phenomenon? Yes. It is because God gave man his agency, and the gift of agency is honored almost without exception. Agency is so honored in the economy of God that no one is forced to do anything *even if it is for their own good.* The most important thing that God's spirit children can do during their mortal probation is to make choices that will lead to eternal life and exaltation. But God is so committed to preserving agency that those choices are never forced on anyone. How remarkable!

And so the Holy Ghost speaks with a still small voice. A louder voice would risk the abrogation of individual agency, which must be honored. Indeed, the still small voice of the Holy Ghost comes only to those who invite it. An uninvited voice, however still and small, would remain contrary to the exercise of individual agency.

The scriptures are replete with the invitation to take some demonstrative action that the Holy Ghost will know is an exercise of agency. One of the most repeated injunctions in the scriptures is that found in Matthew 7:7–8. By some accounts, some variation of this invitation is found in the scriptures more than a hundred times. The verses read, "Ask, and it shall be given you; seek, and ye shall find; knock, and it shall be opened unto you: for every one that asketh receiveth; and he that seeketh findeth; and to him that knocketh it shall be opened." Asking, seeking, and knocking are positive actions that signal to the Holy Ghost that His involvement in testifying of truth will not be in violation of individual agency.

A very interesting confirmation of this important idea is found in the teachings of Nephi, as he concludes his testimony in the Book of Mormon. In 2 Nephi 32, Nephi explains part of the role of the Holy Ghost. He teaches about asking and knocking in these words, "Wherefore, now after I have spoken these words, if ye cannot understand them it will be because ye ask not, neither do ye knock; wherefore, ye are not brought into the light, but must perish in the dark" (2 Nephi 32:4).

Nephi then makes the following observation: "And now I, Nephi, cannot write all the things which were taught among my people; neither am I mighty in writing, like unto speaking; for when a man speaketh by the power of the Holy Ghost the power of the Holy Ghost carrieth it *unto* the hearts of the children of men" (2 Nephi 33:1; emphasis added).

How interesting that the verse describes the Holy Ghost as carrying the word *unto* the hearts of men and not *into* their hearts. The implication is that the Holy Ghost can get the word to the threshold of the heart (meaning *unto*) but it still remains for the person to exercise agency and invite the word *into* the heart.

The person who cannot or will not receive a witness of the truth is often described as "hard hearted." What an apt description. The Holy Ghost will not by force pierce a hardened heart. That would be a violation of agency. He must be invited in.

Earlier in his life, Nephi observed this truth in his interaction with his brothers Laman and Lemuel. Nephi's father, Lehi, had been shown a vision and Nephi, after having experienced essentially the same vision, explained:

And it came to pass that I beheld my brethren, and they were disputing one with another concerning the things which my father had spoken unto them.

For he truly spake many great things unto them, which were hard to be understood, *save a man should inquire of the Lord;* and they being *hard in their hearts,* therefore they did not look unto the Lord as they ought. (1 Nephi 15:2–3; emphasis added)

Nephi recognized that the act of inquiring of the Lord is an exercise of agency that opens the door and allows the Spirit to testify of spiritual truths. This concept is reconfirmed in a conversation Nephi subsequently had with his brothers. The brothers said to Nephi, "Behold, we cannot understand the words which our father hath spoken. . . . And I said unto them: *Have ye inquired of the Lord?* And they said unto me: We have not; for the Lord maketh no such thing known unto us" (1 Nephi 15:7–9; emphasis added).

When Nephi asked his brothers if they had inquired of the Lord, he was asking if they had exercised their agency as part of the process of understanding the things of the Lord. They acknowledged that they had not, arguing that "the Lord maketh no such thing known unto us." Laman and Lemuel clearly misunderstood. They supposed that the Lord would "make" things known unto them.

Nephi, upon hearing their response, reminded them how things work in the economy of the Lord. Nephi said, "Do ye not remember the things which the Lord hath said?—If ye will not harden your hearts, and ask me in faith, believing that ye shall receive, with diligence in keeping my commandments, surely these things shall be made known unto you" (1 Nephi 15:11).

Whether we desire to receive a testimony, receive knowledge, or receive direction in life, the process requires that we exercise agency and invite the Holy Ghost into our hearts and minds. In one sense, this principle may have resulted in some frustration for Nephi. His life certainly would have been easier if he or his father could have forced his brothers to believe his father's words. Parents through the ages can relate to Lehi's and Nephi's difficulty. Neither Lehi, Nephi, nor anyone else could convince Laman and Lemuel of the folly of their thinking. The adage that "a man convinced against his will is of the same opinion still" is a secular expression of the role that will or agency plays in gaining knowledge and wisdom. The secular truth is that an attempt to coerce an individual to believe a certain way will fail. The religious truth is neither God nor the Holy Ghost will ever even try to undermine the agency of man.

After a person is baptized into the Church, that person is confirmed a member of the Church and given the gift of the Holy Ghost. The terminology used—expressing that the Holy Ghost comes as a gift—is relevant to the discussion of agency and the Holy Ghost. A gift can be given, but it must be received to be of value. A gift can remain in a package, unopened, until the receiver chooses to open it. The receiver of the gift must exercise agency and choose to open and receive the gift.

The same is true of the gift of the Holy Ghost. A person can be given the gift of the Holy Ghost by an authorized priesthood holder, but unless the individual exercises agency to receive the gift, the Holy Ghost will not abide with him. The Holy Ghost cannot be imposed. It is not forced but truly is a gift that must be *received.* This is entirely consistent with agency.

Earlier I mentioned that one of the roles of the Holy Ghost is to act as a compliance officer. We learn this concept from the book of Moses: "For by the water ye keep the commandment; *by the Spirit ye are justified,* and by the blood ye are sanctified" (Moses

6:60; emphasis added). The Holy Ghost monitors the justification process. The Holy Ghost can ratify that we have kept the commandments and require no repentance. Or the Holy Ghost can certify that our repentance has been sincere and that forgiveness is warranted because we have followed proper procedures. An individual may be able to deceive a priesthood leader, but the Holy Ghost cannot be deceived with respect to the process of justification or satisfying of the law.

Business firms who wish to deliver an acceptable product to fulfill a contract proactively hire their own compliance officer to make sure that the product meets specifications and is not rejected. A firm without an internal compliance officer risks deluding itself into believing that the product is acceptable until it is too late to meet the required standards. Similarly, we may practice self-justification and try to deliver to our Heavenly Father a flawed product that will not meet the standards of the celestial kingdom. This approach allows us to temporarily avoid the discomfort of addressing our shortcomings. But the scriptures make it clear that it is possible to procrastinate "the day of your salvation until it is everlastingly too late" (Helaman 13:38).

The remedy to this problem is clear. It is to exercise our agency, accept the gift of the Holy Ghost, and actively invite its promptings to help us be in compliance with the commandments of God. This point is beautifully made by Alma:

> And now, my brethren, I wish from the inmost part of my heart, yea, with great anxiety even unto pain, that ye would hearken unto my words, and cast off your sins, and not procrastinate the day of your repentance;
>
> But that ye would humble yourselves before the Lord, and call on his holy name, and watch and pray continually, that ye may not be tempted above that which ye can bear,

and *thus be led by the Holy Spirit, becoming humble, meek, submissive,* patient, full of love and all long-suffering. (Alma 13:27–28; emphasis added)

Alma teaches that we can procrastinate or we can "be led by the Holy Spirit." Being humble, meek, and submissive and being led by the Holy Ghost require that we exercise agency and invite the Holy Ghost to perform His role as compliance officer. He will not force us to accept His help. He cannot, for that would abrogate or compromise the gift of agency, which is not consistent with the plan of redemption.

The relationship of agency and receiving the Holy Ghost is nicely summarized by Nephi:

And it came to pass after I, Nephi, having heard all the words of my father, concerning the things which he saw in a vision, and also the things which he spake by the power of the Holy Ghost, which power he received by faith on the Son of God—and the Son of God was the Messiah who should come—I, Nephi, was desirous also that I might *see, and hear, and know of these things, by the power of the Holy Ghost, which is the gift of God unto all those who diligently seek him,* as well in times of old as in the time that he should manifest himself unto the children of men. (1 Nephi 10:17; emphasis added)

Nephi observes that in times of old (the past), in the time that he should manifest himself unto the children of men (the future), and by inference the time in which he currently lived (the present), God operates in the same mode. The Holy Ghost is the gift of God to all those who exercise their agency and diligently seek Him.

By the power of the Holy Ghost we can "see, and hear, and know of these things."

To make sure we get the point, Nephi reiterates in 1 Nephi 10:19: "For he that diligently seeketh shall find; and the mysteries of God shall be unfolded unto them, by the power of the Holy Ghost, as well in these times as in times of old, and as well in times of old as in times to come; wherefore, the course of the Lord is one eternal round."

How powerful can be our knowledge, how profound can be our understanding, how extensive can be our wisdom if we will diligently exercise agency and seek Him!

God is the same in the past, present, and future. Agency is a gift from God, and it is a gift that was not, is not, and will not be taken back. In honor of the gift of agency, the Holy Ghost speaks with a still small voice. To become like God, man must consciously choose good from evil and do it of his own free will and choice. Help can be invited, but it will not be imposed. Promptings can be heeded or ignored. The more they are heeded, the more often they will come. The less they are heeded the less often they will be offered, even in the most subtle forms.

We can be greatly blessed if we exercise agency and invite the blessings of God. Such is the agency of man and the honor it is accorded by the Holy Ghost.

CHAPTER THIRTEEN

My Will or Thy Will

ASK MOST LATTER-DAY SAINTS whether they would rather exercise their agency on their own behalf or on behalf of the purposes of the Lord, and they will respond in favor of doing the will of the Lord. However, experience and observation suggest that choosing "my will or thy will" presents what some may view as a paradox. Consider the following vignette:

John (not his real name) was a nice looking young man and well spoken. He said he had a normal childhood with loving parents and a regular complement of brothers and sisters. He seemed bright enough; he said he had done well in school and played sports in his local recreation leagues. He had taken a job in a nearby fast-food restaurant and could be depended on to show up to work every day. He was reasonably well groomed, said he didn't drink, smoke, or do drugs, and explained that he had only missed the occasional seminary class while attending high school.

"How old are you?" a questioner asked.

"Twenty-five."

"Are you thinking about going to college?"

"I don't know—maybe."

"Have you thought about serving a mission?"

"Oh, a little I guess."

"Do you have a girlfriend?"

"No, not really."

"Do you see yourself getting married someday?"

"I suppose."

"Do you have any plans for the future?"

"Well, not right now. I'm waiting upon the Lord. I pray often for direction. I want to feel guided in my decisions. I want to be humble and teachable, and I'm prepared to be patient in knowing His will for me. I've heard that the Lord can make more out of someone than that person can make out of himself. I'm willing to wait and see what He does with me."

After such a conversation, some of us would find it a perfect time for a favorite Chinese proverb: "Man stand for long time with mouth open before roast duck fly in."

But what about his premise? Are we not taught to be humble and seek the Lord's will in our lives? What is wrong with waiting upon the Lord and wanting the assurance that what you are doing meets His approval?

The problem is that this young man mistakenly thought that the exercise of agency and an attitude of humility and submission are mutually exclusive. In other words, being humble and seeking heavenly guidance and counsel do not mean that a person should have no plan of his own. In any endeavor, but especially major ones, you want to feel that your agenda, your agency, is not being pursued so single-mindedly that you can't be subject to direction-changing inspiration. On the other hand, it's a mistake to allow yourself to be paralyzed into inactivity by the attitude that since no apparent inspiration has been received, you'll do nothing.

Indeed, sometimes it is only *after* an individual exercises agency and initiative and begins to implement a plan that the Lord intervenes with a ratification or a course correction. In other words, the Lord prefers to work with motion rather than inertness. How the Lord works with us is identical to how the Holy Ghost works with us (they are, after all, one in all things). The Holy Ghost does not ignore our agency by loudly telling us what to do but rather waits until He observes some action on our part that invites His input. Similarly, the Lord honors our agency and waits until we have exercised it and have begun acting on a plan before He offers counsel.

Let me illustrate. One of the keys to success in the mission field is for missionaries to learn to open their mouths "by the way." The Lord taught this principle in the Doctrine and Covenants, as He instructed the first missionaries in this dispensation. He said, "And let them journey from thence *preaching the word by the way.*" And again in the next verse, "Let them go two by two, and thus let them *preach by the way*" (D&C 52:9–10). The injunction to preach and teach *by the way* occurs five more times in section 52 and also is found several times in section 58.

When we arrived in the mission field we were amazed to see how well our missionaries had learned to teach by the way. They opened their mouths on the streets, in the trams, on the buses, and in the parks and public squares. Their favorite activity was to get on a public bus, one at one end and one at the other—always keeping within eyesight and earshot of each other—and work their way from each end toward the middle. They introduced themselves and talked to everyone who would listen. Their cheerful, outgoing natures became well known to the local citizens of every community. One day one of our elders said, "President, a funny thing happened to me last week. We had to run two blocks to catch the train, so I was feeling a little winded when I got on. I just stood at one end catching my breath. I hadn't been standing still very long when a man came up to me, looked at my missionary badge, and said, 'Hey, aren't you supposed to be talking to someone? You'd better get busy!'"

For the most part our missionaries were very successful at finding investigators as they opened their mouths by the way. On occasion, however, our missionaries would fall into a pattern that was not productive. They would decide they wanted to be "guided by the Spirit." So they would wander aimlessly through town talking to people and hope that they would find someone who was interested in listening to their message. It hardly ever worked, and they wondered why.

We asked them to go back to the scriptures and observe that when the Lord instructed the elders to preach by the way, it was always in the context of preaching as they journeyed to a particular destination. We tried to teach the missionaries that they needed a plan. They needed to sit down and exercise their agency—to plan where they were going, why they were going there, and what they were going to do when they got there. They then needed to go forth with energy and enthusiasm to accomplish their plan.

We also explained two important principles to them. The first was that if you don't know where you are going, how can the Lord place in your way someone who is prepared to hear your message? Yes, the Lord is omnipotent, but He does not set aside someone's agency and He almost always works through other mortals to accomplish His ends. Angelic intervention is an extraordinary exception rather than the rule. So, we would tell them, you have to be on your way somewhere—and then one of two things will happen. If you make a specific plan in advance, the Lord can nudge a sincere, truth-seeking person to go to the bus stop or tram line or park where you planned to be. You will then be able to open your mouth by the way and have success.

Or something else will happen that is more subtle. This is the second principle we taught. We said to them that while you are working your plan you may open your mouth by the way and talk to someone that seems interested and even makes an appointment for you to go to their home. You go to their home as part of your plan for the next day, but to your disappointment you find that they are not there. Not only are you disappointed, but you may also be discouraged. After all, you have made a plan, you asked the Lord to bless you in your plan, you are following your plan, and it should be working. This is when the second principle comes into play.

We tried to teach our missionaries that when they went to an appointment and no one was there, instead of turning around and dejectedly going away they should stop and ask themselves, "Why did the Lord bring us here?" And then they should turn and look for the very next person they see. It might be someone walking a dog or working in the flower garden or sitting in a truck on the side of the road or walking along pushing a baby stroller. They should go immediately and talk to that person, because he or she may be why the Lord brought them there. Or they should knock on the very next door they see, because behind that second door and not the first may be the person who has been prepared for their visit.

We tried to explain that people who are prepared are not always or even often in the path of the missionaries. But if the missionaries know where they are going, if they have a plan, the Lord can put an interested individual in their path—or He can put in their path an intermediary who will redirect them to the place where, by opening their mouths, they will be able to teach the individual who is prepared.

How do these notions that we tried to teach the missionaries apply to the rest of us? We would probably all like to be instruments in the Lord's hands to accomplish His purposes. Does exercising our agency in righteousness and having a plan for ourselves help accomplish the purposes of the Lord? I believe the answer is an emphatic *yes!* Of course, we have to exercise our moral agency. Obviously, a plan to steal, lie, be immoral, cheat, or otherwise break God's laws will not be sanctioned by Him.

But what about a plan for learning a trade, getting an education, finding a marriage partner—aren't these self-centered objectives? Isn't this a selfish exercise of agency that makes doing our will more important than doing His? No, the will of the Lord is done by people who are doers. It is His work and glory to bring to pass the immortality and eternal life of man. That is accomplished by doing. It is in the exercise of agency and in the doing that men gain the wisdom, judgment, and power to become as God intended.

It is by design that we have no paid clergy in the Church and that every member, ideally, receives a calling to do something. Sitting idly by and watching someone else is not how we grow in wisdom and spiritual capacity. Magnifying our calling means exercising our agency to seek out what needs to be done and finding a way to do it better and with more love and kindness—all the while seeking the Lord's guidance and help in the process.

President Spencer W. Kimball recognized this concept when he asked Sister Naomi Randall if she would change one word in the song she had written, "I Am a Child of God." When first written, the song said, "teach me all that I must *know* to live with Him some day." President Kimball suggested that the words be changed to "teach me all that I must *do* to live with Him some day."

This principle played out frequently in the life of the Prophet Joseph Smith. Most, if not all, of the revelations Joseph received were in response to problems or questions he encountered in the process of going and doing.

The will of the Lord is that we exercise our agency to be productive according to plans that we prayerfully make and carry out. We need to be educated, develop marketable skills, and do our best to find companions, to be married in the temple, and to raise families. Sometimes, for a variety of reasons, things don't turn out the way we plan. In that case, we go on to plan B and keep doing while we try to better understand the whys and wherefores.

In the process of prayerfully exercising our will to plan and to do, a wonderful thing will happen. We will be like the missionaries teaching by the way. Once we are underway, the Lord will put people in our path whom we can serve, and He will provide opportunities to do His will by using the education, talents, and skills we have developed to bless others and help build His earthly kingdom.

But the key is to get underway. The Lord does not direct inertness; He directs motion. It is easier to steer a moving car than one that is parked. He does not take away our agency to sit and be idle if that is our choice. But once we are in motion, He then can work with us, mold us, and help us find direction and purpose. Once the potter's wheel is in motion the potter can begin to make a beautiful vessel. So it is with our lives in the hands of the Lord.

What about the issue of balance? Can we go too far with our own plans? Can we become so focused and driven that we are impervious to counsel from others, including the Lord? Can our desire for houses, cars, clothes, and vacations—or whatever else—lead us into serious difficulty? Of course! We have all seen examples of willful, prideful use of agency that is antithetical to our best, long-run interests.

That the prideful misuse of agency is a very big issue is attested to by the writings of both ancient and modern apostles and prophets. The pride cycle witnessed by the Book of Mormon prophets is articulately described by Mormon in observations he made in the book of Helaman:

> And thus we can behold how false, and also the unsteadiness of the hearts of the children of men; yea, we can see that the Lord in his great infinite goodness doth bless and prosper those who put their trust in him.
>
> Yea, and we may see at the very time when he doth prosper his people, yea, in the increase of their fields, their flocks and their herds, and in gold, and in silver, and in all manner of precious things of every kind and art; sparing their lives, and delivering them out of the hands of their enemies; softening the hearts of their enemies that they should not declare wars against them; yea, and in fine, doing all things for the welfare and happiness of his people; yea, then is the time that they do harden their hearts, and do forget the Lord their God, and do trample under their feet the Holy One—yea, and this because of their ease, and their exceedingly great prosperity.
>
> And thus we see that except the Lord doth chasten his people with many afflictions, yea, except he doth visit them with death and with terror, and with famine and with all manner of pestilence, they will not remember him.
>
> O how foolish, and how vain, and how evil, and devilish, and how quick to do iniquity, and how slow to do good, are the children of men; yea, how quick to hearken unto the words of the evil one, and to set their hearts upon the vain things of the world!
>
> Yea, how quick to be lifted up in pride; yea, how quick to boast, and do all manner of that which is iniquity; and how slow are they to remember the Lord their God, and

to give ear unto his counsels, yea, how slow to walk in wisdom's paths!

Behold, they do not desire that the Lord their God, who hath created them, should rule and reign over them; notwithstanding his great goodness and his mercy towards them, they do set at naught his counsels, and they will not that he should be their guide. (Helaman 12:1–6)

Mormon observes that men are "quick to be lifted up in pride" and "do not desire that the Lord their God, who hath created them, should rule and reign over them."

Clearly we can use our agency to our own destruction. But in the Lord's love for us, He may intervene in both our collective and individual unbridled use of agency in an attempt to redeem us. We repeatedly read in the Book of Mormon of the form of such intervention.

The Lord explained to Nephi, "If it so be that they [the people of Nephi] rebel against me, they [the Lamanites] shall be a scourge unto thy seed, to stir them up in the ways of remembrance" (1 Nephi 2:24). The warning was reiterated when the Savior visited the Nephites and explained that the Gentiles "shall be a scourge unto the people of this land [the Americas]" (3 Nephi 20:28). The Lord can use one nation or people to cause another nation or people to humble themselves and remember the Lord. The Lord may choose to intervene and seek to alter the agency of a people bent on self-destruction in order to encourage their repentance.

Nevertheless, a people can become so full of pride, so hardened of heart, and so wicked that they are beyond redemption. Such was the case with the people of Nephi in the last days of the prophet Mormon. He explains in these poignant verses:

Behold, I had led them, notwithstanding their wickedness I had led them many times to battle, and had loved them, according to the love of God which was in me, with all my heart; and my soul had been poured out in prayer unto my God all the day long for them; nevertheless, it was without faith, because of the hardness of their hearts. (Mormon 3:12)

For behold, the Spirit of the Lord hath already ceased to strive with their fathers; and they are without Christ and God in the world; and they are driven about as chaff before the wind.

They were once a delightsome people, and they had Christ for their shepherd; yea, they were led even by God the Father.

But now, behold, they are led about by Satan, even as chaff is driven before the wind, or as a vessel is tossed about upon the waves, without sail or anchor, or without anything wherewith to steer her; and even as she is, so are they. (Mormon 5:16–18)

In the end, the people of Nephi had allowed the headstrong use of agency, pride, and wickedness to carry them beyond redemption. The Spirit of the Lord ceased to strive with them, and they became subject to the will of the devil. The people were so bent on self-destruction that finally, after attempting many times to induce them to alter their course and encourage them to choose differently, the Lord gave up on them.

The Lord responds to individuals in the same way as He responds to whole nations or peoples. Before our foolish use of agency leads to our destruction, He intervenes in an attempt to get us to choose differently. Alma observes:

And now, because ye are compelled to be humble blessed are ye; for a man sometimes, if he is compelled to be humble, seeketh repentance; and now surely, whosoever repenteth shall find mercy; and he that findeth mercy and endureth to the end the same shall be saved. (Alma 32:13)

Compulsion can suspend or limit agency, but Alma explains that being compelled to humility sometimes leads to repentance and subsequent salvation. It is important to note that Alma uses the word *sometimes* and not the word *often* or *always* to describe how effective compelled humility turns out to be. Even though humility may be compelled, the repentance is still fully optional. Nevertheless, when an individual responds with repentance to humbling circumstances, a soul may be saved.

Alma goes on to teach another principle. He says:

And now, as I said unto you, that because ye were compelled to be humble ye were blessed, do ye not suppose that they are more blessed who truly humble themselves because of the word?

Yea, he that truly humbleth himself, and repenteth of his sins, and endureth to the end, the same shall be blessed—yea, much more blessed than they who are compelled to be humble because of their exceeding poverty.

Therefore, blessed are they who humble themselves without being compelled to be humble; or rather, in other words, blessed is he that believeth in the word of God, and is baptized without stubbornness of heart. (Alma 32:14–16)

Alma makes the point that though a person may be blessed when compelled to be humble, the greater blessing awaits those who choose to humble themselves without being compelled. The simple truth is that great blessings are promised to those who correctly use agency.

In the end, the question of "my will or Thy will" in the exercise of agency is clear. The Lord expects us to exercise our agency and our own initiative, to be prayerful and seek guidance as we develop a plan, and to get underway. It is not intended that He should command in all things. "For he that is compelled in all things, the same is a slothful and not a wise servant; wherefore he receiveth no reward" (D&C 58:26).

Once we are underway, if we are humble and exercise agency to ask for help, we will be gently prompted and guided so that our will and the will of the Lord are congruent and compatible. If we become headstrong, willful, or hardhearted and have not already made such foolish decisions that we are beyond help, we may be compelled to be humble and be rescued from the chains of the devil, which could cause us to lose our agency forever. But this is a course involving serious risk, because forced humility and repentance only works "sometimes."

The Lord's greatest blessings are reserved for those who go forward with faith, who choose to do good, who seek inspiration but are not motionless in its absence, who pray always (see Alma 34:27), and who thereby gain the wisdom, judgment, and godlike attributes that our mortal experience was intended to bestow. "Get on your knees and pray and stand on your feet and do His will and put your trust and faith in Him and God will bless you" (President Gordon B. Hinckley, regional conference, Santiago, Chile, 26 April 1999).

Agency, Faith, and Miracles

Going forward with faith and humility with a plan that allows for redirection from the Lord also opens the door to another wonderful possibility that brings agency into play.

Moroni included a very interesting and even provocative comment in his abridgment of the book of Ether. He wrote, "For if there be no faith among the children of men God can do no miracle among them" (Ether 12:12).

Upon first encountering this verse, one may be tempted to agree and continue reading. However, it is useful to pause and ponder what is implied by the statement. To say that "God can do no miracle" suggests that somehow God is *not* all powerful. It implies that at least under some conditions He is powerless. Is that what we believe? I think not.

Several possibilities present themselves. We may posit that God has to follow certain rules that govern His actions. We read in Alma, "Now the work of justice could not be destroyed; if so, God would cease to be God" (Alma 42:13). The principle is that justice and adherence to the law are precepts or rules that God cannot break without ceasing to be God. This raises the question, Is requiring that faith precede a miracle a law or rule that God must comply with?

Two examples come quickly to mind that seem to illustrate situations where miracles occurred in the absence of faith. The first is the miraculous appearance of Jesus to Saul of Tarsus (Acts 9:1–8). Saul (Paul) was an enemy to the Church and its members and took part in the martyrdom of Stephen. He could not be described as a man of faith—certainly not prior to his conversion, in any case. Alma the Younger was in a very similar situation regarding his own lack of faith and the persecution of Church members. It could be argued that Alma's conversion was a miracle that followed his father's faith and was not related to Alma the Younger's own faithlessness (Mosiah 27:8–24). Nevertheless, these two examples cast some doubt on the notion that faith is an immutable law that restricts God in the same manner as justice.

Another way of explaining the meaning behind Ether 12:12

presents itself. It may be that where "there be no faith among the children of men," God can do no miracle, not because He is powerless to do so, but because *He chooses not to do so.* If that were to be the case, the next question would be, Why does He choose not to do so?

Perhaps in the absence of faith, God chooses not to perform miracles in order to honor our agency. We have learned how important agency is in the economy of God. The war in heaven was fought over it, our eternal salvation is determined by it, and most of what we experience in life can be explained by it.

So what is the relationship between agency, faith, and miracles? Faith is a principle of action. Action is an expression of agency. When we exercise faith and act on that faith, we are expressing our will to the Lord. In the *Lectures on Faith* the Prophet Joseph wrote that faith is "the principle of action in all intelligent beings." Continuing, he said:

> If men were duly to consider themselves, and turn their thoughts and reflections to the operations of their own minds, they would readily discover that it is faith, and faith only, which is the moving cause of all action in them; and without it both mind and body would be in a state of inactivity, and all their exertions would cease, both physical and mental.
>
> Were this class to go back and reflect upon the history of their lives, from the period of their first recollection, and ask themselves what principle excited them to action, or what gave them energy and activity in all their lawful avocations, callings, and pursuits, what would be the answer? Would it not be that it was the assurance which they had of the existence of things which they had not seen as yet? Was it not the hope which you had, in consequence

of your belief in the existence of unseen things, which stimulated you to action and exertion in order to obtain them? Are you not dependent on your faith or belief for the acquisition of all knowledge, wisdom, and intelligence? Would you exert yourselves to obtain wisdom and intelligence unless you did believe that you could obtain them? (*Lectures on Faith* [Salt Lake City: Deseret Book, 1985], 1:9–11)

The Prophet explains eloquently how faith is a principle of action. Faith is an action that signals to God what our will is. A miracle must be our will before it can be His will. We let him know through faith that He will not abrogate our agency should He choose to perform a miracle in our lives. However, signaling through our faith that we welcome a miracle is a necessary but not sufficient condition that a miracle be experienced. The miracle must also be the will of the Lord and fulfill His purposes.

Not only does God typically choose not to perform miracles in the absence of a faith-driven action on our part, but there is ample evidence from the scriptures that uninvited miracles often have no effectiveness. The lives and experiences of Laman and Lemuel attest that signs, wonders, and visitations generally have no lasting effect on hardened hearts.

We have suggested that a necessary condition for a miracle is to signal to the Lord by our faith and our actions that a miracle in our lives would be in keeping with our agency. We've also noted that such a miracle must be the will of the Lord. But is it possible to go a step further? Is it possible for us to exercise agency in such a way as to go beyond *inviting* a miraculous outcome to a position where we are able to *dictate* an outcome? To put it another way, can we choose a course of action that would "bind the Lord"?

In the Doctrine and Covenants we read, "I, the Lord, am

bound when ye do what I say; but when ye do not what I say, ye have no promise" (D&C 82:10). We should not doubt that the Lord is bound by the promises *He* makes. His promises of a glorious resurrection, of eternal life, of forgiveness through repentance, and of exaltation in the celestial kingdom are sure and are made to every one of the Father's children. Further, when He gives a specific commandment with a specific promise attached, He binds himself to grant the promised blessing when we are obedient. But it would be incorrect to suppose that He could be bound by some unilateral action that we would take. We cannot dictate to the Lord.

We are often counseled to petition the Lord mightily for a particular outcome. And we might in our zeal wish that we could go beyond petitioning and guarantee that the Lord would do exactly as we asked. But experience teaches that, once all the data has been received, we are grateful that the Lord's will was not bound by our nearsighted petitioning.

We can exercise our best judgment and pray for a particular outcome based on that judgment, but every prayer ought to include the phrase, "Nevertheless, not my will but Thy will be done." We should be grateful that we cannot force our will on any given situation when we have such limited knowledge of all the outcomes that would be experienced both by ourselves and by others.

In sum, it is important to consider the principle of agency when considering the issue of "my will or Thy will." Elder Maxwell has taught eloquently about true discipleship and the blessings that come from submitting our will to the will of the Lord. (See "Willing to Submit," *Not My Will, but Thine* [Salt Lake City: Deseret Book, 2008], 93–120.) But it is the Lord's will that we exercise our individual agency and learn the lessons that this mortal life was designed to teach. As we pursue righteous objectives and pray for guidance, we can be directed in ways that will fulfill the purposes of the Lord. We can plan and act and be directed by the Lord so that our will becomes more and more in tune with His will. We can seek and knock and expect the door to be opened. We can show our Father in Heaven, by our faith and actions, that a miracle in our lives, if it be His will, would surely be our will as well. If we are prayerful and seek the Lord's counsel, we will experience the incalculable blessings that attend the righteous use of agency. In our seeking we will find that agency is an extraordinary gift of inestimable value embedded in a perfect plan!

CHAPTER FOURTEEN

Intergenerational Agency

IT WAS A SATURDAY morning in January, and Elder W. Craig Zwick, a member of the Area Presidency, and I were several hours from the mission home in Geneva when the cell phone rang. It was one of my missionary assistants, who exclaimed with excitement, "President, guess what—Sister Dudouit wants to be baptized!"

I knew the assistants had been teaching this wonderful young Swiss woman, who had a promising law career and who had been making slow but steady progress in preparing for Church membership. "That's marvelous, Elder," I said.

"But, President, she wants to be baptized tomorrow." We had a rule in the mission that baptism interviews had to precede the baptism by at least twenty-four hours. We agreed that there was still time for a Saturday interview and a Sunday baptism.

The elder then said, "But, President, she wants to be baptized in the lake!" A baptism in the lake was a little more problematic. The air temperature in Geneva where Lac Leman (Lake Geneva) is located had not been much above freezing for many days. The water in the lake was not frozen, but it was cold enough that some ice formed each night along the lakeshore and then melted during the day. But if Sister Dudouit wanted to be baptized in the lake in the middle of January, we would make it happen.

All the necessary arrangements were made, and the next day, Sunday, we met at about 5:00 P.M. at the mission home, which was located some three hundred yards from the lakeshore. Sister Dudouit and the missionary who would perform the baptism were dressed in white; we all bundled up in our winter coats and hats and made the short walk to the lake. In the baptismal party were Sister Dudouit's parents and sisters, several missionaries, President and Sister Zwick, and Sister Nadauld and me.

The scene was simply spectacular. The waters of the lake were glassy smooth in the gathering twilight. Across the lake on the opposite shore could be seen the twinkling lights of the homes that dotted the Swiss hillsides. In the distance behind the hills loomed the pure white French Alps, with Mont Blanc, Europe's highest mountain.

With this serene and exquisitely beautiful scene as a backdrop, Sister Dudouit and the baptizing missionary entered the lake without hesitation and began walking out into the freezing water. As the missionary raised his right hand to the square, the whole panorama was indelibly etched in each of our memories. The baptismal prayer was pronounced, and in a single graceful motion Sister Dudouit was lowered gently beneath the frigid water and brought forth again clean and pure. We bundled them both up in warm blankets and took them back to the mission home.

If the story were to end there, it would be an account of an impressively beautiful baptism. But there is much more. The story of the Dudouit family began many years earlier. Brother and Sister Dudouit (the parents of the woman being baptized) had been very young members of the Church in Switzerland. While still in their teens they fell in love and were married in the Swiss Temple. Sister Dudouit became a nurse and worked, while Brother Dudouit studied medicine and ultimately became a doctor with a successful practice. Along the way five children, four girls and a boy, were born into the family. Since the Dudouit parents had been married in the temple, each of the children was born in the covenant. But Brother and Sister Dudouit became inactive in the Church, and none of the children was taught the gospel and none was baptized.

After many years the Spirit of the Lord and the sealing power began to move upon the family. Within a short time, four of the five children were taught the gospel and baptized. The first was a daughter who was visiting in southern France and met the missionaries on the street. She was taught and returned home to be baptized in Lac Leman in June. One day a few months later, the Geneva missionaries, responding to a knock on the door, found the Dudouit father and a fourteen-year-old daughter, who was introduced to the missionaries as eager to be taught and baptized. Independently, the Dudouit son met the missionaries in England, where he joined the Church. The baptism of the son resulted in his desire to serve a mission. Appropriately, he was called to serve in England, where he himself had joined the Church. The parents were touched by the son's mission call and concluded that they should prepare and accompany their son when he went to the temple prior to his departure. The January baptism we witnessed was just the continuation of an ongoing story.

After Sister Dudouit and the baptizing missionary changed back into their Sunday clothes, we were all warmed with cups of delicious Swiss hot chocolate. Sister Dudouit was then surrounded by loving priesthood leaders, who placed hands on her head and, with her father as voice, confirmed her a member of the Church and gave her the gift of the Holy Ghost.

Elder Zwick, knowing something of the history of the family, then asked Sister Dudouit if she would like to speak to her brother, who was serving a mission in England. She said she would. Elder Zwick contacted the mission president and was able in a matter of minutes to have the missionary brother on the phone. Imagine his surprise and delight! He knew nothing of his sister's investigation, conversion, and within-the-hour baptism. After Sister Dudouit had talked for several minutes, Elder Zwick offered the phone to the missionary's mother and then his father.

What a wonderful and tender scene unfolded that beautiful winter evening in Switzerland. The sealing power exercised in behalf of a young couple so long before had reached out through time and space and brought a child born in the covenant back into that sacred covenant relationship.

The story of the Dudouit family is the intergenerational story of the gospel. It is a story of hope. It is the story of the power of the sealing ordinance to reach out through time and space and bring those born in the covenant back into that sacred relationship. It is the story of a young couple who made the right choice early in life, lost their way, then returned to right choices when given a second chance.

Not all stories of families have this happy outcome. I do not know why the Dudouit family was so blessed. Indeed, there are yet other chapters and important gospel-oriented decisions to be made by the newly baptized generation of Dudouits if the blessings of salvation are to be passed on to the coming generations.

It is fitting to conclude our discussion of agency by addressing the intergenerational effects of the exercise of our Father's great gift. Upon consideration, one of the most disconcerting aspects of agency is the influence our actions might have, not just on ourselves, but on others. We can assess the direct effects, but there are many indirect effects that we are unaware of and cannot measure. Those most directly and indirectly affected through time, for better or worse, are our immediate family members.

The scriptures offer a very sobering commentary on this issue. In the second of the ten commandments that Moses received from the Lord we read, "Thou shalt not bow down thyself unto them [graven images], nor serve them: for I the Lord thy God am a jealous God, *visiting the iniquity of the fathers upon the children unto the third and fourth generation* of them that hate me" (Deuteronomy 5:9; emphasis added).

We have been given the privilege of choosing right from wrong, good from evil, and righteousness from iniquity. If we choose iniquity we risk the likelihood that those we should hold most dear, our children, grandchildren, and great-grandchildren, will suffer greatly from our misuse of agency.

Many are the families that can point to a sad example of this principle. A choice by an individual to ignore the teachings of the prophets and apostles, to break important commandments, or simply to be offended can lead to whole generations being estranged from the Church and denied the blessings of the gospel. By contrast, the righteous choices of one individual can bless the lives of countless descendants.

We should all worry about the effect our actions and choices will have through time. When we presided over the Switzerland Geneva Mission we learned that missionaries are not immune to these worries. Indeed, they are prone to worry, as they should, about whether their work and sacrifice will make any lasting difference in anyone's life. They may see many, few, or no converts, but they will not necessarily know, in any of the cases, the long-term fruits of their labors. But it turns out that every missionary can have a wonderful intergenerational arithmetic working in their behalf.

Let me explain. It turns out that the one convert each missionary can count on is himself or herself. It soon dawns on mission presidents, as well, that their most important converts are the individual missionaries they are blessed to serve with.

With that as a beginning, the intergenerational arithmetic becomes quite amazing. A missionary who returns from two years of service with a deep, abiding testimony of the Savior and a desire to live a life of discipleship may not perceive the long-term impact of his personal conversion. But soon he or she will likely have an eternal companion. Then children come into the home, and they are taught to love the Lord. In the twinkling of an eye, it would seem, there are grandchildren. In a few short years the missionary, who was one person, is now surrounded by and has influence on children, spouses, and grandchildren of twenty, thirty, or forty in number.

A mission president and spouse may serve with 300 missionaries during the course of their service. In a few short years those 300 missionaries could account for 9,000 faithful Church members. Fifty thousand missionaries Churchwide could in forty years represent a potential 1.5 million converted descendants. A decade's worth of missionaries (25,000 per year) could in forty years constitute a force for good of 7.5 million persons.

Each of us must ponder this arithmetic with soberness. The gift of agency was not lightly given; it cannot be lightly received. We cannot be cavalier in our exercise of agency. We cannot say that our decisions are no one else's business. We will not be exempt from the intergenerational effects of our use of agency. It is not part of the plan!

The scriptures contain several great intergenerational stories. The most important of these is the story of Abraham, Isaac, Jacob, and the twelve tribes of Israel. The covenants that were made with Abraham and extended through the generations, even unto our day, play a fundamental role in God's plan for extending the blessings of the gospel to the peoples of the earth. But the Book of Mormon contains another example that is perhaps easier for today's Latter-day Saint families to relate to.

One way to organize all the history contained in the Book of Mormon is to reconstitute it as basically four family histories. If we set aside the book of Ether and the story of the Jaredites as a special case, we are left with the families of Lehi, Mosiah, Alma, and Mormon. One of the potentially confusing aspects of these four family stories is the duplication of names. For example, there are multiple Lehis, Nephis, Almas, and Helamans that have to be sorted out and kept straight. One way we do that in modern society is to give them "family" names. In the spirit of "likening" the scriptures to ourselves, I have found it useful to assign last names to at least some of the Book of Mormon families.

For example, the last name I usually assign to the first family in the book, that of Lehi, is *Cohen.* Cohen is a nice Jewish family name, and Lehi's family is a nice Jewish family that emigrated to America. Giving the family a last name helps me realize that Lehi, Nephi, Sam, Joseph, Laman, Lemuel, Jacob, Enos, Jarom, and Omni are all "Cohens." In this way, Lehi and Nephi Cohen are easily distinguished from other Lehis and Nephis who lived hundreds of years later.

The second family is the four-generation family of Mosiah, Benjamin, Mosiah, and the sons of Mosiah. Even though they are also direct descendants of Lehi, for the purposes of this exercise I will call them the Brown family. They are several hundred years removed from their roots in the Holy Land, and any common family name serves equally well to identify their relationship to each other and to the other three main families.

The fourth family is that of Mormon and Moroni, and

because of the uniqueness of their names and smallness of the family I'm able to keep track of them without assigning a family name.

I must confess that the third family is my favorite. I have taken to calling them the Johnson family and identify them as Alma Johnson, Alma Johnson Jr., Helaman Johnson, Helaman Johnson Jr., Nephi Johnson, and Nephi Johnson Jr. Giving these six Book of Mormon prophets a last name has provided some wonderful insights into the whole Book of Mormon. For one thing, the last name makes it clear that the six are a succession of fathers and sons all belonging to the same family. Remarkably, the story of these six fathers and sons of the Johnson family constitutes more than half of the total pages of the Book of Mormon. Once the Johnson family is understood, the history of half the book is under control.

The family story begins with Alma Johnson's conversion by Abinadi and has as its high point the visit of the Savior, who is welcomed by Nephi Johnson Jr. in the land of Bountiful. The story of the six generations unfolds over a time period that is easy to comprehend. The 180-odd years from Alma Johnson's conversion to Nephi Johnson's welcoming the Savior is almost exactly the same as the six generations (assuming thirty years per generation) from the Prophet Joseph's first vision until today.

Essentially the writers of the family, at least those to whom Mormon looked for source material, are the juniors. Thus the book of Alma is mostly about Alma Johnson Jr. And the writers and subjects of the books of Helaman and Third Nephi are respectively Helaman Johnson Jr. and Nephi Johnson Jr.

With that background, we can look at the Book of Mormon for a valuable truth about the intergenerational impact of agency. Alma Johnson was converted by Abinadi as he listened to Abinadi talk about the Savior and the beautiful feet upon the mountain. The account is found in the Book of Mosiah. Abinadi is brought before the king and his priests, and they ask him to explain the meaning of the words found in Isaiah: "How beautiful upon the mountains are the feet of him that bringeth good tidings; that publisheth peace; that bringeth good tidings of good; that publisheth salvation; that saith unto Zion, Thy God reigneth" (Mosiah 12:21; Isaiah 52:7). Abinadi proceeds to give an eloquent and powerful discourse on the Law of Moses, the need for a Savior, and the great blessings of the atonement and the resurrection. Abinadi's words sank deep into the heart of Alma. Indeed, he must have either transcribed them directly as they were being spoken or memorized and rewritten them a short time later, because we have them in great, first-person detail.

The doctrine of the atonement and of the beautiful feet upon the mountain that sunk so deeply into his heart was undoubtedly taught by Alma Johnson to his son Alma Johnson Jr. The richness of the doctrine found in the book of Alma and the testimony of its writer, Alma Johnson Jr., are a testament to that assertion. Similarly, I believe that Alma Johnson Jr. taught his son Helaman Johnson about the Savior and His beautiful feet. Indeed, I believe that the testimony of the Savior was taught unceasingly by father to son through the six generations of the Johnson family.

The power of that teaching prepared the sixth of the Johnsons to receive the Savior at the temple in the land of Bountiful. The image of the beautiful feet upon the mountain and the significance of the Savior's atonement were indelibly engraved on Nephi Johnson Jr.'s mind. When he had the opportunity, he acted on that testimony: "And Nephi arose and went forth, and bowed himself before the Lord and did kiss his feet" (3 Nephi 11:19). In doing so, he was kissing the beautiful feet upon the mountain that he knew were bringing salvation to him, his family, and his people.

The story of the Johnson family is the story of successive

generations of fathers and sons choosing the Savior. By contrast, consider the poignant words of Omni (Cohen) found in the book of Omni. Omni was the son of Jarom, the grandson of Enos, the great-grandson of Jacob, and the great-great-grandson of Lehi. So he was a fifth-generation Cohen. In Omni 1:2 he says of himself, "Wherefore, in my days, I would that ye should know that I fought much with the sword to preserve my people, the Nephites, from falling into the hands of their enemies, the Lamanites. *But behold, I of myself am a wicked man, and I have not kept the statutes and the commandments of the Lord as I ought to have done*" (emphasis added).

Thus the Cohen family devotion to the Lord essentially lasted only four generations. And though the plates were retained by subsequent Cohens for several more generations, they had to be passed on to the family of Mosiah before the workings of the Lord were again recorded by a Nephite family.

The Cohen and Johnson families of the Book of Mormon are examples of the intergenerational impact of agency through successive priesthood leaders. However, there is a very interesting contemporary example of intergenerational agency through a righteous woman. Consider the family of Mary Fielding Smith, the wife of Hyrum Smith. Both Joseph the Prophet and Hyrum his brother were martyred on June 27, 1844. From that day forward their families were in the hands of their respective wives. Mary Fielding Smith, still a widow, left Nauvoo in the fall of 1846 and in 1848 crossed the plains to the Salt Lake Valley. The account of her experiences during the journey is one of extraordinary faith, determination, and heroism. Her single-minded devotion to the Lord has blessed many generations and tens of thousands of descendants. On February 13, 2000, the anniversary of Hyrum Smith's two hundredth birthday, Elder M. Russell Ballard (a direct descendent of Hyrum) observed, "President Hinckley, as nearly as we can estimate, and it certainly is an approximate estimate, we think there are about 31,000 living descendants of Hyrum Smith. Probably somewhere in the proximity of 35,000 total descendants of Hyrum. When you compare that with the approximate estimated posterity of the Prophet Joseph, his would number somewhere between eight hundred to nine hundred" (Elder M. Russell Ballard, talk in Assembly Hall, Temple Square, Salt Lake City).

In chapter one of this book we read the account of a conversation between Enoch and God, recorded in the Book of Moses. Enoch was unable to understand why God would weep as He looked over His spirit children on the earth. In revisiting that conversation we read,

> The Lord said unto Enoch: Behold these thy brethren; they are the workmanship of mine own hands, and I gave unto them their knowledge, in the day I created them; and in the Garden of Eden, gave I unto man his agency;
>
> And unto thy brethren have I said, and also given commandment, that they should love one another, *and that they should choose me, their Father;* but behold, they are without affection, and they hate their own blood. (Moses 7:32–33)

God was weeping because His children chose to misuse the gift of agency He had given them. His desire—as would be that of any parent—was that His children love one another and choose to return to His presence. Alma Johnson and the five generations that followed him understood. Each in succession, they chose to love the Lord and teach their children to love Him as well. They were preparing a righteous generation of their family for the day when that generation could stand in the presence of the Savior and welcome Him.

That is all that our Heavenly Father expects of each of us—
that we exercise our agency wisely—that we choose Him, and prepare a generation to receive His Son when He comes again in His
glory.

We must not lose sight of that objective. Ours is a generation
blessed above any other when it comes to the exercise of agency
and the unbelievable number of choices available to most Church
members. I was struck with a simple example of this notion one
day some years ago. We had a twenty-year-old young man and his
fifteen-year-old sister as house guests; they had come from Russia
to spend several weeks with us. We took them with us one morning to our neighborhood grocery store in Bountiful. When they
walked into the store their mouths literally gaped open. For several minutes they walked up and down the aisles just shaking their
heads and saying nothing. When they finally overcame being
speechless and we could coax some words out of them, they
explained that they had never seen so many vegetables, so many
fruits, so much meat, so many things to drink, and so many other
things they didn't even have names for.

We can choose to recreate in dozens of ways and choose among
hundreds of cars to drive and thousands of clothes to wear—not
to mention movies to watch, books to read, text messages to send,
Internet sites to visit, and on and on and on. I presume our
Heavenly Father is not unhappy about the incredible fabric and
texture of our lives. Our challenge is to separate out of the fabric
and texture and color the more important choices from those that
are less important or even insignificant.

Moral agency is not about a red or blue car, an apple or a pear,
snow skiing or snowmobiling, or a calf-length or knee-length skirt.

Imbedded in the thousands of modern choices is the real
essence of agency. It has not been altered through all the generations of man on the earth. God's view of agency is that we learn to

know good from evil and right from wrong, that we teach our children to exercise moral agency, that we recognize that God, our Heavenly Father, is the embodiment of good and right, and that we choose Him. Our success in mortality is not determined by what we choose to eat, wear, drive, or live in. Our success is determined by how well we follow the plan of redemption, which is the basis for our mortal sojourn. The essence of the plan is that we learn to choose good from evil, that we have faith in the atonement and apply it in our lives. In a sense, the depth of our understanding of the plan can be measured by how well we teach agency and the atonement to our children, so that we, with them, might be blessed through the generations.

If we choose the Lord and teach our children to choose the Lord, He will, as John the Revelator promised, dry our tears and take away all our sorrows (Revelation 21:4). The gift of agency is an extraordinary blessing. Truly, it is the first great gift. Its wise use will bless our lives eternally. I pray it will be so for each of us.

Index

Accountability, 49–56

Actions: good and evil and, 37; learning God's will through, 167–71, 176; faith and, 178–80. *See also* Behavior

Adam: agency given to, 25; exercises agency, 27–28; learns plan of redemption, 28–29; brings death into world, 31–33

Agency: as gift, 1–2, 25, 31; answers life questions, 3; definition and essential elements of, 4–7; understanding, 7–10, 42; as gift given in premortality, 14–15; Satan encourages refusing, 17–18; finding joy in, 32–33; taking full advantage of, 33–34; meanings and interpretations of, 35–36; uncertainty and, 108–10; normal distribution in outcomes and, 115–18; efficiency of, 121–24; faith and uncertainty and, 130–37; of earth, 141–48; veil and, 148–51; Holy Ghost respects, 158–61; accepting gift of Holy Ghost and, 161–64; God's views on, 194–95.

Alcohol, 49–52

Alternatives, as essential element of agency, 6–7

Ambulance, 58–60

Athletes, 35–36

Atonement: faith in, 19; Jesus Christ promises to fulfill, 19; saves men from Fall, 31–32; as price of agency, 39–43; receiving comfort through, 42–43; agency comes through, 57; saves us from bad choices, 58–61; as incentive for continued learning, 126

Attitude, Viktor E. Frankl on, 67–68

Ballard, M. Russell, on descendants of Hyrum and Joseph Smith, 192–93

197